SORTED

Kate Kray

BLAKE

Published by Blake Publishing Ltd,
3 Bramber Court, 2 Bramber Road,
London W14 9PB, England

First published in hardback in Great Britain 1997
Published in paperback 1998

ISBN 1 85782 370 2

British Library Cataloguing-in-Publication Data:
A catalogue record for this book is available from
the British Library.

Typeset by BCP

Printed and bound in Finland by
WSOY - Book Printing Division

3 5 7 9 10 8 6 4 2

For Dolly,

with love

Contents

I think of my ex-husband nearly every day. I have very fond memories of him and our time together.

I know he would approve of what I've written because all these stories come from him.

I would like to thank all the people who have helped me with this book; all have contributed in their own way. Special thanks to Bernard Black, for his kind permission to use some rare photographs.

The 'firm friends' for sharing their personal stories about Ron. Harry for inspiration and support; Priscilla O'Reilly for typing and computer skills; Mandy Bruce for guidance; Terry Garwood, the computer wizard; Freda Bolton —my friend, without her dedication this book would never have been written.

Last, but by no means least, 'His Nibs' for just being there!

Love, Kate

Prologue

It was billed as the biggest funeral the country had seen since Sir Winston Churchill's in 1965.

The coffin was carried in a Victorian glass coach, drawn by six black horses wearing plumed head-dresses and followed by a fleet of 46 black limousines all smothered in enormous wreaths.

The procession wound through the streets of London's East End and it took two hours to make the journey from St Matthew's Church in Bethnal Green to the cemetery in Chingford.

An estimated 50,000 people lined the route — some to pay their respects, some to say a fond farewell, others simply to gawp. But this was no hero they were saying goodbye to, but one of the most famous villains of modern times. Many of the mourners were villains, too, men who had spent much of their life behind bars. The chief mourner was actually still being detained in one of Her Majesty's prisons, but was let out especially for the occasion — he was the deceased's twin brother, Reggie.

For in the coffin, being carried to his last resting place, were the skin and bones of the legendary gangster Ronnie Kray.

On 17 March 1995, at the age of 61, Ronnie Kray had died suddenly of a heart-attack in Wexham Park Hospital after serving 27 years of his 30-year life sentence in the top-security prison hospital for the criminally insane, Broadmoor.

Two days before the extraordinary spectacle of his funeral, a young, blonde woman, smartly dressed in a pin-striped suit that Ronnie had always admired, hiding her tear-puffed eyes behind enormous dark glasses and carrying an equally outsized heart-shaped wreath, was quickly ushered into an East End funeral parlour by the burly security guards who were, at his brother's instructions, keeping vigil for Kray.

The woman was Kate Kray who had come to say a private goodbye to her ex-husband Ron.

Ronnie and Kate Kray were married in Broadmoor in November 1989. As even the bride and the groom admitted, it was probably the most bizarre love-match in Britain.

He was in his 50s, a paranoid schizophrenic and self-confessed homosexual, a gangster, murderer and torturer.

She was in her early 30s, a glamorous, bright and bubbly divorcée who was a successful businesswoman in her own right owning chauffeur-driven car and kissogram companies.

But, to much surprise, the marriage lasted five years and there was a strong and loving bond between the couple even after they divorced in the year of Ronnie's death.

Kate became his most trusted friend and visited or phoned him every day. She ran errands for him on the outside, enabling him to keep on top of business and rake in hundreds of thousands of pounds even though he was incarcerated. She was his go-between, his link to friends in the underworld. Kray's letters were censored, his phonecalls were tapped and his every move watched. But Kate was a free agent — and she was a very loyal wife.

But most of all, she was his confidante. With Kate he could unburden himself of the secrets of his brutal past, and tell the truth about his existence in Broadmoor, safe in the knowledge that she would never reveal all she knew until after his death.

Ronnie Kray had only three years of his life sentence left to serve when he died. His greatest fear was that he would die in Broadmoor, but he was enough of a realist to appreciate that it was unlikely that he would ever be released.

No Home Secretary, he said, would risk their political career by signing the documents authorising his freedom.

To many, Kray's crimes were too barbaric, his madness too deeply entrenched, he showed little or no remorse for his crimes — quite the contrary was true, in fact — and he was simply too famous.

To the police, and many ordinary law-abiding citizens, Ronnie Kray and his twin Reggie were violent villains, nothing more nor less.

But to many others they were seen, especially in their 1960s heyday, as latter-day Robin Hoods who ruled their 'manor' with a rod of iron or sometimes a gun, knife or red-hot poker, making it safe for ordinary folk to walk the streets and go about their everyday business unhindered and unmugged. After all, said the same folk, they were only violent to their 'own kind' — and Ronnie was always good to his mum.

The Kray twins grew up, with their elder brother Charlie, in Vallance Road, Bethnal Green — later dubbed by the locals 'Fort Vallance' — in a family dominated by strong women; their much adored mum, Violet, and their Aunt Rose, both considerable influences on their early lives.

In those days, if you lived in the East End and you wanted to make anything of yourself, you either became a boxer or a villain. The twins tried both with enthusiasm. They loved boxing and had a natural talent for it. By the time they were 16, they'd both won some impressive fights and had been written about in the *Daily Mirror*.

But, even then, they didn't confine their fighting to the ring. Locally, they were already notorious. They slept with knives and machetes under their beds, they had their own gang and they'd been barred from most of the dance halls and cinemas in the neighbourhood for causing trouble. They were only 16 when they made their débuts at the Old Bailey in the famous Number One Court, charged with causing grievous bodily harm to three other young men during a gang fight.

It was only thanks to the intervention of a friend, the local vicar who ran a youth club and appeared as a character witness on their behalf, that they were acquitted.

They continued to box, both turning professional when they were 17, but by that time their alternative career — as villains — was already beginning to blossom. Anything was considered fair game, as long as it brought in the money. They stole lorryloads of goods: fruit, furniture, alcohol and cigarettes, even aeroplane parts from an airbase. Other scams involved arranging exemption certificates from National Service for 18-year-olds and selling duty-free watches smuggled into the East End docks.

Their career was briefly interrupted by a spell of National Service, although the twins quickly decided that their army life wasn't for them and they were jailed for desertion. But, free once again, they pursued their 'business' ventures with renewed vigour.

They went into the club business and protection rackets and that formed the core of their operations for many years to come. Their first big venture was The Regal, a billiard hall in Mile End. The owner was having trouble with local thugs who were smashing the place up on an almost daily basis. He turned to the Krays for 'protection' and the trouble soon stopped.

'It was very simple,' the twins said. 'The punters knew that if there was any trouble, if anything got broken, Ron and I would simply break their bones.'

Soon local bookies, pubs, drinking clubs and gambling bosses were all paying the Krays a cut of their takings in return for their 'protection'.

The Krays were now respected — but feared. They gathered their own crowd of trusted 'employees' around them who were known as The Firm. The Krays, themselves, played the roles of Godfathers. They had become a law unto themselves and people crossed them at their peril.

They enforced their 'law' with beatings and torture and Ronnie, who was showing the first signs of paranoia, was particularly violent. One man who was not among the mourners at Ronnie Kray's funeral was EastEnder Lennie Hamilton. Years before, in a club, Ronnie had overheard him call a girl 'love'. That was enough to send Ronnie berserk and he attacked Hamilton with a red-hot poker, leaving him almost blind in his left eye.

Both Ronnie and Reggie served time in prison for their activities — Ronnie was sentenced at the Old Bailey to three years' imprisonment for grievous bodily harm and also pleaded guilty to carrying a loaded revolver, and Reggie spent a year in Wandsworth Prison after he was found guilty of demanding money with menaces.

But, despite the violence — or maybe because of it — there was a glamour about the twins which attracted people to them like moths to a light bulb. They converted a large, rambling house in Bow Road into their own exclusive nightclub, the Double R, and they were very proud of it — 'a place where a man could take his mother, wife or fiancée for a drink in a respectable atmosphere,' said Reggie.

The Double R was highly successful and brought in more and more cash, as did the twins' other sidelines: the protection rackets, the second-hand car businesses, the money laundering and the backing for 'jobs' carried out by other villains which brought them profit for doing very little at all.

In the late 1950s and early 1960s, the twins seemed invincible. They opened other clubs, sometimes under their own names and several where they chose to stay in the background as silent partners. At one stage, they were running an illegal gambling club immediately opposite Bow Police Station, but their tentacles also reached from the East into the West End.

Esmerelda's Barn was a posh gambling club in Knightsbridge, 'up West', and that was soon joined by The Kentucky in Stepney. Showbusiness stars flocked to the clubs. It wasn't the plush red carpets, gold mirrors and gold 'antique' furniture which attracted them — they liked the idea that they were living dangerously mixing with all these villains, and the Krays in particular. Diana Dors, Shirley Bassey, Judy Garland, Sophie Tucker and Winifred Atwell were all photographed enjoying a drink with the twins. And, among their friends, Ronnie and Reggie counted politicians, aristocracy and the most famous boxers of the time.

They both enjoyed the fame and the champagne lifestyle. They dressed the part in flashy made-to-measure suits and drove expensive cars. Their success was intoxicating but their private lives were troubled.

Behind the scenes they lived simply either back with their mum in Vallance Road or in a series of rented flats. Reggie, who always had an eye for a pretty girl, fell head-over-heels for a beautiful young woman called Frances Shea, and they were married against her parents' wishes in April 1965. Two years later, she committed suicide.

Ronnie, a bisexual, had many affairs with pretty young men. Reggie was increasingly worried about Ronnie's illness which, by now, was obvious, as he became more and more unstable.

But 'business' boomed. They bought a big house in the country, a racehorse for their mum and travelled extensively to Germany, Italy, France, Ibiza, Casablanca, Tangier (from where they were extradited) and Turkey (where Ron spent much of his time in the local brothel).

Back home, the police were becoming increasingly frustrated. As the Krays' fame grew, national newspapers, among others, were pushing for a clamp-down on the twins and other London gangs. But it seemed impossible to make any charges stick. The Krays were untouchable.

In many ways, the tide turned against the Krays

in 1966. Ronnie became involved in a business deal with the famous peer of the realm and former Conservative MP, Lord Boothby. There were rumours that the two were having a homosexual affair. Boothby sued — and won — a libel suit against IPC, the publishers of *Mirror Newspapers*, but the damage had been done.

All the publicity surrounding the case was just what the Krays didn't need. The police were determined to act and, slowly but surely, began to build their case against the twins.

At the same time, the Krays became involved in a feud with the Richardsons, a South London gang led by Charlie Richardson, whom the twins knew from their army days, and his brother, Eddie. There was a gang fight during which one of The Firm was shot.

The feud escalated as various members of the Richardson gang were arrested. But one who escaped the police was a man called George Cornell. Ronnie, by now, according to friends, quite seriously mentally ill, took the law into his own hands.

On 9 March 1966 — almost three years to the day before being sentenced to life imprisonment at the Old Bailey, Ronnie went to The Blind Beggar Pub in the East End where Cornell was drinking and calmly shot him dead through the head. Famously, the record on the jukebox jammed and blasted out one line again and again: 'The sun ain't going to shine any more, the sun ain't going to shine any more ...'

Ronnie and Reggie were both taken in for questioning but were released — eyewitnesses refused to talk.

If anything, the episode enhanced, at least temporarily, the twins' reputation and it was business as usual. They even managed to spring a villain called Frank Mitchell — known as the 'Mad

Axeman' for obvious reasons — from Dartmoor prison. He later mysteriously disappeared.

The twins were warned that two senior police officers — Nipper Read and Fred Gerrard — had been assigned to their case full-time with instructions to 'get the Krays' whatever, or however long, it took.

But Ronnie and Reggie laughed off the threat and bought themselves two pet snakes which they fed with live mice and called Nipper and Gerrard.

In 1967, the twins were becoming increasingly irritated by a villain called Jack 'The Hat' McVitie, a frequent drunk who had taken the liberty of brandishing a sawn-off shotgun and threatening members in one of their clubs. They agreed that McVitie had to go. He was duly invited to a party where the twins and other members of The Firm were waiting for him.

Reggie pointed a .32 automatic at McVitie but the gun jammed. So, while other members of The Firm held a struggling and terrified McVitie, Reggie stabbed him in the neck, face and chest until he was dead.

On 8 May 1968, the twins were out on the town having a few drinks at the Astor Club in Berkely Square. They were well aware that they were being watched by the police — they easily spotted the plain- clothed officers mingling with the other guests at the club — but they shrugged it off. They were quite used to being under surveillance.

What they didn't know was that for months, behind the scenes, Read and Gerrard had been slowly and painstakingly building a rock-solid case against the Krays.

With patience and perseverance, they had managed to persuade vital witnesses that their case against the Krays was now water-tight. The Krays were finished. Many people took some persuading but, to the everlasting disgust of the twins, some of The Firm 'turned grass'.

At 6.00am on the morning of 9 May 1968, Nipper Read and his team, all carrying .45 calibre Webleys, kicked down the front door of Ron's flat at Credra Court in Bunhill Road, Walthamstow, while the twins were asleep. Ronnie and Reggie were arrested and both were charged with the murders of Cornell, McVitie and, later, Frank Mitchell. Other charges included fraud, demanding money with menaces and grievous bodily harm.

What followed was a nerve-racking time for those Eastenders who had decided to talk. The twins were safely locked up awaiting trial but, as one Cockney said: 'If people talk to the police and the twins get off again, they'll have to send the plague carts into Bethnal Green and shout: "Bring out your dead!"'

But this time the twins didn't get off. Both were found guilty at the Old Bailey and were sentenced to life imprisonment with a recommendation that they did not serve less than 30 years apiece.

Reggie was initially sent to Durham jail. After a series of fights in prison, Ronnie was finally certified insane and sent to Broadmoor Hospital where he stayed until his death in 1995.

But the twins' imprisonment was by no means the end of the Kray story. Even today, nearly 30 years on, they are still big box office and the name Kray can still command respect from some, and fear from others.

Ronnie did his best to maintain standards — visitors to Broadmoor never saw him wearing anything but a made-to-measure suit, usually

Cashmere, matched with a crisp white shirt, silk tie, hand-made shoes, gold cuff-links and gold Rolex watch. And he carried on with business as best he could, given the circumstances, raking in hundreds of thousands of pounds over the years in one crooked way or another.

'If you wanted to bring a smile to Ronnie's face,' said his wife, Kate, 'all you had to do was bring him a bit of business.'

Even though they were divorced, Kate admits that she still misses the man she affectionately called 'Him Inside'. To her, he was 'a very special man, a funny old sod, but special'.

To millions more he has become a legend, Britain's most famous gangster, a figure almost of fiction. And many of the stories that have been told about Ronnie Kray are, according to Kate Kray, just that — fiction.

'So much crap has been written about Ronnie and Reggie,' says Kate. 'Some of it amused Ron, some of it really irritated him. We talked a lot and he was always honest with me. He trusted me. I know what really went on, both before he went into prison and afterwards.

'He told me his secrets. He knew I would never tell anyone while he was alive — he never worried about that, he didn't need to.

But sometimes he would have a joke with me. He'd tell me something in confidence and then he'd say: 'Pay attention, me old Dutch! When I'm gone that's going to make a good story for a book of yours one day ...'

This is that book ...

M B, June 1997

1

To Hell and Back

'Ronnie Kray will, today, be transferred to Broadmoor Hospital for the criminally insane.'

Those were the words that stung Ronnie Kray's ears early in the morning on 25 July 1979 as he listened to the BBC radio news on a small transistor radio. He was in Parkhurst Prison on the Isle of Wight at the time, in the punishment block, deep in his madness. Nobody knew what to do with him and nobody could control him. He told me the screws had tried everything — beating him, putting him in a strait-jacket — nothing had worked. He was naked, laying on the floor with just a blanket and his small radio for comfort.

The screws were cruel bastards. They taunted him through the spy hole in the door.

'You're being nutted off, Ronnie. How do you like that?'

Ron never said a word. He didn't give a damn. He knew they couldn't hurt him anymore. Three whole months they had kept him in solitary confinement. Three months. It must have seemed like three years. A weaker person would have gone mad being kept in solitary that long. Ron was already suffering from a mental problem. Three months of being kept in the dark, alone and naked, in what they called the 'strongbox', tipped him over the edge. The strongbox was a room, a square room. The whole thing was made of concrete, with a little bed in the middle. It wasn't really a bed, just a slab of cold stone.

The only person to show Ron any compassion or kindness was a medical officer called David Cooper. He gave him the small transistor radio and allowed him to keep it in the strongbox.

After that living hell, it's a wonder Ron was alive. He later told me that when he was eventually transferred to Broadmoor, he was the maddest he had ever been in his entire life.

The journey from Parkhurst to Broadmoor was a long one. Ron remembered it well. He said it was a bright sunny day. He was handcuffed and shoved into the back of a white prison van. Five screws sat in the back with him. The van boarded the ferry from Ryde to Portsmouth. Ron took a deep breath and held it. The air was different. Fresher. Seagulls squawked. The noise was deafening. The screws laughed and joked all the way. Ron said nothing. The van pulled off the ferry and down the motorway to Crowthorne, Berkshire.

Ron peered out of the small window on the side of the van. It was a hot afternoon in July. People were out in their cars, some were towing caravans, they looked happy. Deep inside, Ron envied them. The van pulled off the motorway into what seemed like a big park. The guards started moving about inside the van. Ron looked out of the small window again and saw a big sign on a white board: 'Broadmoor Special Hospital. Private Property'.

The van laboured as it climbed the steep hill towards the hospital The sun flickered through the tree-lined drive and Ron caught a glimpse of the hospital for the first time. It was a big, imposing Victorian building. It looked every bit an asylum.

Ron was amazed that the bricks were orange — bright orange. The walls were high. The huge wooden gates opened and swallowed the prison van.

Once inside the small courtyard, Ron was struck by the silence. He expected to see patients, doctors and nurses, the hustle and bustle of a hospital. But there was nothing — just silence.

He was taken directly to the admission ward. There he was stripped, searched internally and bathed in the compulsory six inches of water.

He never said a word as they shaved his head and covered him in a foul smelling lice powder. He was given a white paper boiler suit to wear and was escorted into a cell where the door slammed and bolted behind him. He slumped down on the small bed and pulled the itchy grey blanket over his shoulders.

During those early weeks and months he was seen by an endless stream of doctors, psychologists, education officers and social workers and was assessed by them all. Finally, he was placed on the appropriate medication. Four times a day he took Stemetol capsules to quieten his nerves. He was given Disipal for the side-effects caused by the Stemetol, which sometimes made his limbs shake. Every fortnight, he had an injection of Modicate, which is a drug specifically to curb the symptoms of schizophrenia. It took three months for his condition to be brought under control.

Eventually, he was well enough to be transferred on to a ward in the mainstream hospital. All the wards in Broadmoor are named after towns and counties in England: Taunton, Kent, Suffolk. Ron was taken to Somerset House.

Ron settled down on the ward quickly. However, the daily routine was hard for him to get used to at first. Every day was the same. Unlock at 7.00am. Slop out. Wash and shave, then wait in line while the razors are counted. They can't take any chances in case the patients have suicidal tendencies or, even worse, attempt to kill again.

That was the main event of the day. After that, they were taken to the day-room where they sat until 9.00pm unless they had a visit. In the day-room, there were five rows of chairs across the room, and a television set at the end, which was constantly blaring. Down the side of the room was a line of blue chairs. These were for the staff. They watched the patients' every move and listened to every conversation. Ron stayed on Somerset Ward for the next 12 years, leaving the ward only for visits and the occasional hospital check-up.

Ron didn't mind. One thing is for sure, he was better off there and considered himself luckier than when he was in Parkhurst. He was allowed more visits in Broadmoor than when he was in prison. In fact, he could have two visits a day if he wanted. In Parkhurst, he was allowed only two visits a month. Also, he could wear his own clothes in Broadmoor. The food was better, too. But there was a down side.

Norfolk House was the punishment block at Broadmoor. Its name would strike fear into anyone who had been unlucky enough to be detained there.

At first, Ron was reluctant to talk about his experience on Norfolk House. His face tightened and he scowled.

'Nothing in this world can compare to the punishment block in Broadmoor,' he whispered.

I was shocked. I imagined that prison would be tougher. Ron shook his head.

' Norfolk House is your worst nightmare come true.'

The look on Ron's face said it all. I was intrigued.

'Why is it a nightmare, Ron?' I asked.

He lowered his eyes. It was as if he was too embarrassed to tell me. Gently, I rubbed his back to reassure him.

'Tell me, Ron. Nothing can be that bad.'

He took the last drag of his cigarette and slowly stubbed it out in the ash tray. He turned his head to the side and exhaled the smoke and sighed.

'OK, if you want to know then I'll tell you.'

I watched him carefully as he started to talk.

'I'd got into an argument with another patient. I can't remember what about. I got mad. Bloody mad. I hit him. The punch broke his jaw. Alarm bells were sounded.

'Before I knew it, I was bundled to the ground by five or six burly officers. I kicked, punched and bit every fucking one of the dirty bastards. But I didn't stand a chance.

'They dragged me along the corridor by my legs. They didn't walk, they ran with me. Everyone that was standing in the corridor got out of the way. The officers tried to drag me into a cell but I held on to the door-frame. Three of them tugged at my legs. They pulled so hard that my trousers came down around my knees. I held on to that fucking door-frame for dear life. One of the dirty bastards kicked my hands. Still I wouldn't let go. He got annoyed and bent my fingers so far back I thought they would snap. I screamed out in agony and let go of the door-frame. The three officers that were pulling my legs fell backwards. The cell door slammed shut. Five of the fuckers grabbed me. I tried to fight them off. I didn't stand a chance. They threw me on to a bed. Well, I say a bed it was more like an examination table. It had thick leather straps at the side with big shiny buckles. I struggled like fuck but they overpowered me and strapped my arms to the side of the table. Next, my legs were buckled in place.

'I couldn't move. The officers were worn out wrestling with me. They slumped against the wall to catch their breath.

'I wriggled and wriggled, pulling at the straps. They laughed.

' "You ain't going nowhere, Ron." '

'I spat at them and cursed them. But they wouldn't stop laughing. The cell door swung open. In walked a doctor. He said, "Remove his clothes."

'The dirty bastards took my clothes off so I was naked.'

For a moment, Ron paused. I looked at him. He was angry, upset. He poured his chilled lager and lit another fag.

'You don't have to tell me any more if you don't want to,' I said.

He shook his head. 'You wanted to know so I'll tell you. The doctor turned to a small trolley that was directly behind him and pulled on a pair of surgical gloves. He didn't look at me. Again, I tugged at the straps. The doctor motioned to the officers.

' "Hold him still."

'He approached me holding a syringe. A screw held the top of my arm. I tried to bite him. Someone grabbed my head. The doctor flicked the syringe. Small droplets of a clear liquid exploded from the end of the needle. He plunged the syringe into my arm. I closed my eyes tight and held my breath. I felt the cold fluid run through my veins. My heart started to pound like a drum. I felt dizzy, sick.

'I tried to fight the effect of the drug, but it was no good. The screws that were holding me let go. I clenched my fists and pulled at the leather straps that were holding me down. My back arched and I went into a convulsion.

'What happened to me over the next five months is vague. I still have flashbacks. I must have been going in and out of consciousness. I remember terrible hallucinations. My most vivid recollections are of devils and demons screeching and screaming at me.

'Watching the ceiling getting closer and closer to my face, the fear of being trapped in that room for ever was probably the most fearsome experience of my entire life. Colours, those bright flashing colours so bright they stabbed my eyes whether opened or closed — it made no difference. I felt fear, uncontrollable fear like I've never felt before. Loneliness. I don't remember being unstrapped the whole time I was in that room, but I do remember the nurses giving me more mind-blowing drugs.

I looked at Ron. Remembering it all made his face almost screw up in pain. He sipped at his drink. He looked tired.

'I never want to go back to Norfolk,' he whispered. 'Sometimes, in my head, I can still hear the cries of other patients. They used to scream.'

I didn't know what to say. I just looked at him

and those sad eyes. There was a silence. Neither of us said anything for a minute or two.

Five months they kept Ron on Norfolk — the House of Correction, the staff call it. Five long months. He must have gone to hell and back. It was a nightmare, one that was to haunt him for the rest of his life. I suppose that's why there used to be little or no trouble in Broadmoor. The threat of Norfolk must have loomed over every inmate.

Ron often talked about Broadmoor. He already knew a lot about the place long before he was transferred there. It was way back in 1963 when Ron first went there. That time it was to visit a good friend, Roy Shaw. Roy told Ron that it wasn't a bad place to do bird. It was ironic that he ended up there later.

Another friend of Ron's called Nobby Clark pre-warned Ron, saying that Broadmoor could be heaven or hell, it just depended on you. He should know. Nobby did his time the hard way. Nobby was a wiry old goat. He had long grey hair and a long grey beard with bright twinkling eyes. He had a troubled life and was one crazy bastard. While he was serving time in Parkhurst, he speared another inmate, stabbing him while he was lying in the bath.

He was transferred to Broadmoor and was never released. He had a heart-attack and died there. Ron told me the story of Nobby several times. He never forgot his warning that it could be heaven or hell.

In the first few years of Ron's time in Broadmoor, he wanted to find out all about the place. He got a book out of the hospital library. It was out of date but that didn't matter to Ron. The book was written in the early 1950s by a man called Ralph Partridge. It was called *Broadmoor: A History of Criminal Lunacy and Its Problems*.

It didn't paint a true picture of how Broadmoor is today, but it was a starting point. It had photographs and conversations with older patients and staff at the hospital. In the early days it was barbaric. The patients were kept like animals.

This intrigued Ron enough to encourage him to find out more about the asylum. Broadmoor was built by a man called Joshua Jebb. He must have been a latter-day builder — a Victorian Mr Barratt. It was originally built because of a madman with a gun who had tried to kill the King of England. They had nowhere to put him. They said he was totally mad. He had to be to try to kill the King. But what to do with him? Make an example of him. But how? The answer was to build an asylum for him so he could spend the rest of his miserable life there — hence Broadmoor. By a strange twist of fate, the King later became mad himself.

Crowthorne in Berkshire was chosen because, in those days, it was thought that the fresh air would be therapeutic for the lunatics. As if a raving nutter would care less what the air was like. Boredom is the biggest enemy in Broadmoor. The patients just have so much time to kill, if you pardon the pun.

If you aren't paranoid when you go into Broadmoor, you soon will be. The staff watch your every move. Observation by nursing staff is a key factor in the security. It has to be. The patients are, after all, the most dangerous in Britain. Certain patients are 'grasses' and feed the staff with information thinking that it will win them favour. It's just tittle-tattle really, nothing of any importance. It's not as if they are informing on some elaborate escape plan.

It is rare that anyone escapes from inside Broadmoor. Most escapes occur while patients are on outside work parties. All movement throughout the hospital, by patients and staff, is watched closely.

The whole hospital is saturated with video cameras which are linked to a central control room.

Staff always know where every patient is, at any time of the day or night. If they need to check out an individual, it's easy — they hunt them down with the camera. Big Brother is always watching you.

The walls around Broadmoor are the highest around any prison in Europe, higher than the Berlin Wall used to be. The wall is designed to have a psychological effect on the inmates. At its lowest point it is 30ft high. If you had thoughts of clambering over it, you might just as well forget it, unless you're Superman.

Just to make doubly sure, the wall has an infra-red beam running the length of it as a further security measure. The beam is so sensitive it can be broken by the smallest creature, setting off an immediate alert in the control tower. Officers with dogs patrol the perimeter constantly. When the alarm is sounded, the whole hospital grinds to a halt. The patients are head-counted back to their cells until the panic is over. It happens often. If someone is missing, the hospital goes on red alert. The siren is sounded to warn the surrounding area. Mothers gather up their children in case it's not a false alarm, hoping and praying that it's not a child murderer on the loose. A photograph of the escapee is faxed to all the police stations in the area. Road-blocks are set up within a 15-mile radius. Broadmoor is like Nazi concentration camp. It has to be.

All Broadmoor patients are suffering from psychotic disorders, many are schizophrenics. Most schizophrenics have ancestors or relations with mental disorders. In Ron's case, his mental problems can be traced back to his great-grandfather, Critcha Lee, who was a gypsy and cattle-dealer from Bermondsey and died in Claybury Madhouse. Ron's grandfather's brother, who was called Jewy, also died there. Ron was a paranoid schizophrenic. He struggled with the illness for many, many years — maybe for most of his life.

On one of our visits, I asked Ron to describe what schizophrenia was and, more importantly, how it felt. It was rare that Ron would talk about his illness. But this particular day he felt good and explained in great detail.

What he said shocked me — it must have been a battle which he had to fight every day. He said that it was the voices in his head that drove him mad. He described it vividly. It was like having a radio on in his mind, like background music never going away, a continuous noise he couldn't turn off. But, instead of listening to his favourite song, the radio in his head whispered evil things: 'He's going to kill you, kill him first.'

The voices never stopped. The drugs helped a bit but, he said, they just seemed to turn the radio down, so he strained to hear the voices. He then had to concentrate really hard just to catch what the voices were saying. He said that he could be on a visit or talking to someone on the ward, but he never heard a word they said. He was too busy listening to the evil voices.

It was a constant struggle to decide what was reality and what was not — what was evil and what was good.

When Ron was feeling like that, more often than not he would cancel his visits. He did this for two reasons. One, he didn't want anyone to see him like that; and two, he didn't want to distrust his friends.

He explained to me early on in our relationship that, from time to time, he may not want to see me or anyone else. I got used to his ways just like any normal married couple. After a while, I began to see the signs myself when Ron was 'going into one' as he put it. I could tell straight away. It was his eyes. They were sort of blank. Empty. Dead.

Ron knew himself when he wasn't feeling right. He would see the doctor and ask him to increase or decrease his medication.

The drugs helped the bad dreams and the depression, but what nothing could cure was the terrible feeling of loneliness. When Ron felt like that, it was best just to leave him alone. That's the way he preferred it.

Usually in prisons, grasses and sex offenders are segregated. In Broadmoor it doesn't happen like that. Ron said that if he was to slap every nonce (sex offender) he came across in Broadmoor, then he would be slapping someone every five minutes. Everyone in Broadmoor has committed a horrendous crime, but the difference there is that the offender is suffering from some sort of psychological disorder. Ron hated sex offenders and child killers and hated mixing with them, but he had no choice. Even so, he soon let it be known that such beasts should stay away from him and they got the message.

In the autumn of 1990, things changed for the better in Ron's life. He was going to move from the old Somerset House block that had been his home for 12 years to a brand-new block called Oxford House. Ron was told he would be on Henley Ward, on the first floor.

He was glad and had been looking forward to the move for months. In Somerset House he had to slop out every morning as he didn't have his own toilet. All the toilets and washing facilities were at the end of the corridor, four sinks for thirty patients. The toilets had no privacy; neither did their cells. In the new block, all the cells had a toilet and wash basin. They even had a built-in wardrobe.

But the biggest thing that pleased Ron was the window. For the first time in nearly 25 years, there were no bars on the windows because the glass is unbreakable.

Every year, a patient is entitled to a tribunal and every three years it is compulsory that the patient attends. Ron considered these a waste of time. I wanted to attend them but he told me not to bother because there was no way they were going to release him. A tribunal is made up of a judge, a doctor and a member of the public.

Very few patients are discharged by a tribunal. The only way out of section 65 is to convince the psychiatrist looking after you that you are fit to be discharged. He then has to persuade the Home Secretary. No Home Secretary in his right mind was going to put his political career on the line by agreeing to release Ron.

But just because Ron couldn't get out, didn't mean he couldn't go on with business. I did many things for him. I didn't mind, that was all part of being married.

Then, late one evening, I got a phonecall asking me to visit him urgently. I drove to Broadmoor at the crack of dawn trying to avoid the rush-hour traffic. Ron was on good form.

'You look happy,' I said.

He was in no mood for idle chat.

'Never mind all that,' he said. 'I want you to go to Waterlooville in Hampshire.'

He was happy. So I knew it was to do with money. Nothing made Ron happier than when he had a nice few quid coming.

'I want you to pick up £85,000.' He laughed.

My jaw dropped open. I could have tucked my chin in my knickers.

'Eighty-five grand!' I couldn't believe it.

'Yeah, in notes,' he purred.

I was used to picking up large amounts of cash for Ron, but this was an unusually large amount, even for him. I didn't know what it was for, or where it came from. I didn't ask. Ron didn't explain; he just gave me a long list of names where he wanted the cash to go.

On this occasion, he decided that he would send someone with me to ride shotgun. I can't remember who he was, all I can remember is he was big and mean.

Ron insisted that I follow his instructions to the letter. I travelled to Hampshire, wondering if it was going to be a wasted journey. Eight-five grand was a lot of money.

I couldn't help thinking to myself that it must have been some blag for Ron's cut to be that big.

I did hope nothing would go wrong. There had been the odd occasion when I've been to collect money for him, and when I had got there something had gone wrong or someone had been nicked. Whatever the reason, the money wasn't there and, oh boy, did Ron get the needle.

It was a long journey to Waterlooville, and I just hoped this was not going to be a wasted trip although Ron seemed very confident.

I parked my car in the small car park at the rear of the bank . As I walked into the bank shadowed by my minder, I was humming the song 'Me and My

Shadow' under my breath. We must have looked a right pair! The bank was full. We queued. I gave the cashier all the relevant paperwork. The young girl behind the counter looked at me and then at my shadow.

'Wait here, Mrs Kray,' she said gingerly.

She went to the Manager's office. I dread to think what she said. His door opened — he stuck his head out. He looked at me, then at my shadow, and shut the door again. The door opened for a second time. The cashier and the Manager came out of the office together.

They mumbled to each other, looked at me, then mumbled again. I looked around the bank trying to appear inconspicuous. The more I tried to look innocent, the more guilty I felt. At that point, it did cross my mind to wonder exactly where the money was coming from. But then I thought, if the money isn't kosher, Ron would never allow me to go and get it. The Manager broke my thoughts.

'Mrs Kray.'

My heart leapt into my mouth.

'How would you like the money?' he said.

I stuttered. 'Er ... Er ... Large notes, please.'

It took the cashier and the Manager ages to count the money in front of me. I couldn't wait to get out of that bank. I got back into my car and drove out of Waterlooville.

A few miles up the small country lane, I pulled the car over into a lay-by. I opened a can of coke and took a large gulp. It should have been something stronger — sometimes it's a pity I don't drink alcohol. I offered the can to my minder. He shook his head, turning his nose up.

'Let's have a sort out,' he urged.

I pulled the money bag out from the glove

compartment and banged it down on the dashboard. It was a huge bag. I peered inside. It stunk. Slowly, I started to count the money into small piles. One hundred. Two hundred. Three hundred. When the piles were complete, I stuck a coloured 'post-it' note on the top with the name of each person who was going to receive the cash.

It took ages to sort out £85,000. But who's complaining? I kept looking at my watch. I knew Ron would be wondering if things had gone smoothly.

My instructions were that once I had got the cash and counted it out into bundles, I had to visit Ron. I didn't want to be late, as I knew he would be wondering if things were all right.

That was probably my own doing because I had teased him previously saying that once I had got the cash I was going to run off and send him a postcard from a sunny desert island.

I laughed. So did he. Thank God.

I dashed up the M3 to reach Ron for the afternoon visit. I just made the visiting hall by 2.30pm. Eagerly, Ron was waiting.

I walked into the hall. He stood up and looked at me trying to gauge my expression. I raised my eyes to the heavens, shook my head and threw my hands in the air in defeat. He looked angry and pissed off. I realised it was not the best time to have a joke with him.

I smiled, winked and rubbed my hands together.

'You little minx,' he laughed. 'You got it, ain't ya?'

'Of course I got it,' I replied. He hugged me tight.

'Where the fuck is it?'

'In the glove compartment of my car, that's where.'

'But ... but ... you can't ...' he spluttered.

With my hand held high, I stopped him in his tracks, like a policeman holding up the traffic.

'It's all right. Calm down. It's being baby-sat by the fucking shadow.'

'That's all right then.' That seemed to pacify him.

We spent the whole visit sorting out the money. I spent the entire next day being Father Christmas distributing it. Ron eventually got round to telling me where the £85,000 came from.

It was legit. It was paid to Ron from the Fugitive film company as proceeds from the hit film *The Krays*, starring the Kemp brothers from the pop group Spandau Ballet. £85,000 was the first payment — more was due but, unfortunately for Reg and Ron, the company went bust.

I was astonished at the amount of money that flowed into the Kray coffers, even though the two key players were locked away for 30 years.

For five years I was drawn into the network doing cash drops and making pay-outs to friends for services rendered. I had one mission in life at that time — to help make Ronnie's life inside as comfortable as possible.

I was amazed that the authorities did not seem to realise Ronnie was operating his rackets inside Broadmoor. It was done under their noses.

I suppose they didn't realise what was going on. I'm glad, because that was what kept Ron going. He would try any business venture, no matter how far-fetched, in order to make money. He was the best money-getter I have ever met or am ever likely to meet. He was a tough businessman, but fair. There weren't any villains whom Ron didn't know. His black address book was the *Who's Who* of the underworld. I automatically assumed that all the gangsters knew each other. Not true. They all knew

Ron, but not each other.

All the gangsters looked up to Ronnie while he was in Broadmoor, and treated him with the utmost respect. He was the main man, and what he wanted was done!

Robbery, murder, intimidation ... Ronnie ran it all. He even organised or financed fake car discs, travellers cheque scams, counterfeit designer label clothes ... you name it, he was into it. Villains from all over the country used to visit him looking for finances for a job. If they wanted to do a bank job, they would tell him the area they wanted to do it in, and Ron would sort it out with the boss of the local 'firm', so no one's toes got trodden on. He'd tell them, 'It's down to me,' and because they respected him, they'd never object. If the boys needed anything, like sawn-off shotguns, or a stolen car with a new identity (they call it a 'ringer') then Ronnie would sort it out through his contacts.

He could arrange anything they needed. They would tell him what they had planned and how much they could make. Ron would either give them the nod or tell them to forget it. If he liked it, he would tell the organisers exactly what his cut was to be. There was no room for discussion. Take it or leave it.

I saw tens of thousands pour in week after week ... and pour out again. Of course, none of it went directly to him in Broadmoor, but everything he wanted was paid for out of his cut and was brought in for him.

The bulk of Ron's money never passed through Broadmoor and, for years, I became Ron's trusted confidante. I dealt with his money. I had his account books. He trusted me to get cash out for him to take it here, take it there, pay so and so, pick something up for someone. I never really knew what all the transactions were about.

Some of the names Ronnie used were coded, and it was obvious they weren't straight dealings. I didn't want to know. If I didn't know anything then I couldn't say anything.

I knew I was becoming drawn into dangerous territory, but I suppose that was one of his attractions. Ron was a very exciting man.

Once I had completed a drop, I normally didn't see Ron until the next day but I always rung him at 8.00pm every single evening.

We used a code to communicate because Ron was not allowed to use the telephone then, so I spoke to the nurses. I used to ring up and ask if Ron was OK. Ron would always stand outside the small office on the ward waiting for my call.

I was never late ringing him. It didn't matter where I was in the world, I would make sure Ron got his call at 8.00pm. I didn't say much. I would just ask if he was all right. The voice on the end of the line would say, 'Yes, he is OK. Just fine.'

Ron would know it was me. He would put his head round the door and ask if I had picked his suit up from the cleaners. The screw would relay the message and by the tone of the voice I realised they considered it trivial.

If only they realised the importance of the message. If I replied yes, I had picked up his suit, I would hear them call out to Ron.

'Yes, Ron, she has picked up your suit.'

He would call back, 'Oh good. Tell her I said goodnight and God bless.' He would walk away with a smile on his face, confident of the fact that everything had gone smoothly.

On the other hand, if I said that I hadn't picked

up his suit from the cleaners, he would still say 'goodnight and God bless', but walk away cursing.

The nurses never took much notice. There was always someone swearing or a crazy outburst of some sort. It was an everyday occurrence, one that Ron got used to.

On one particular occasion, he had had a boring morning. He was fed up. It was dinnertime. The patients filed in to get their meals. Ron sat down at the table. It was just another day, the same as all the rest. No one spoke. They were only interested in their food. All of a sudden, one of the elderly patients stood up, pulled his trousers and pants down to his ankles and, at the top of his voice, yelled, 'Fuck my arse.'

Nobody stopped eating. Nobody looked up. A nurse who was sitting chatting in the corner put his teacup down, sighed and tutted.

'Come on, pull your trousers up.'

The old patient was adamant. 'It was you,' he pointed at the nurse. 'You're God and it was you that fucked me up the arse last night.'

The nurse shook his head. 'Yeah. That's right. It was lovely. Now eat your fucking dinner.'

The old boy pulled his trousers up, sat down, and continued to eat his dinner. Just another day in the loony bin.

Broadmoor houses the maddest people in the country. Not only are they insane but, even worse, they are criminally insane, meaning that they have committed a terrible crime.

No ordinary, run-of-the-mill lunatic goes to Broadmoor. The inmates are really only the ones with nothing to lose, as they know they are never going to be released. So how do the staff remain in control?

Apart from the threat of the punishment block, there are other control methods, like electric shock treatment. Ron had this treatment on many occasions, but not always with an anaesthetic. He told me that it makes you lose your memory for a few days afterwards.

He said it was barbaric when he first had the treatment. He walked into the room voluntarily, and even climbed on to the bed on his own. When the officers held him down, only then did he realise it was a big mistake. They forced a big rubber clamp into his mouth to stop him biting his tongue. The doctor attached electrodes to his forehead. He told me of the searing pain and how it felt as though his brain was being fried.

The doctors claim that they do this because if the patient is depressed or violent it calms them down. Ron said it works. The only down-side is that it makes you forgetful and, if done without an anaesthetic, it hurts like hell.

I haven't got any proof, and Ron didn't have any either, but he was convinced that the patients in Broadmoor were used as guinea pigs to test new drugs. It seems feasible. Why not?

The patients have no knowledge of their drugs; all they know is that they have to take them. If they don't they are forcibly injected.

Three patients have died in drug-related incidents in the past eight years. An inquest into one of the patients called Orville Blackwood heard how he died within three minutes of being given a drug to control his bad behaviour.

Blackwood, who was suffering from schizophrenia and depression, was given the drug when he became violent on Abingdon Ward. At his inquest, the pathologist said he did not believe that

Blackwood died from natural causes; he said his death was due to heart failure caused by calming drugs.

Most of the patients are in Broadmoor for years and the only visitors are their parents, who are normally elderly. Once they die, the patients have nobody. They are completely alone.

One of the patients in Broadmoor has been there for 60 years for stealing just a pint of milk, but they can't let him out because he is completely institutionalised. When he dies, chances are that he will be buried in the confines of Broadmoor. It's sad. But the fact is, who really cares?

You are, in fact, paid to go to visit someone in Broadmoor. It is not a lot, just expenses. No one is means tested.

Everyone is treated the same whether you are an elderly lady with a small income who visits your wayward son or daughter for 20 years, or a gangster's wife, driving a gold Rolls Royce. Everybody is entitled to the money offered. I always refused payment. I think that money in the Health Service could be better spent. It is astounding.

One patient I know, whom I will not name, had tattoos all over his arms and legs and the NHS paid for their removal.

*　　　*　　　*

There are three hospitals for the criminally insane: Rampton, Park Lane in Liverpool and, of course, Broadmoor.

Ron was a wise old fox and soon realised how to work the system in order to secure a reasonable lifestyle.

There is a hospital shop in Broadmoor. If a

patient needs anything, you have to buy it from the mini-market.

The patient is allowed to go into the shop with you and anything purchased goes into a box and is taken on to the patient's ward.

Each patient is allowed to have an account which has to be paid off monthly. Nobody is allowed to handle real money.

Patients use social security money, plus hospital wages and gifts from family and friends to buy sweets, toothpaste, cigarettes and newspapers. All the newspapers are censored by the hospital and any articles which could upset patients are cut out. Ron very rarely bought newspapers but he did shop at the mini-market.

Once, Ron did not settle his bill for over a year. He was told that, until the bill was settled in full, he could not have anything thing else. His bill was just under £7,000. Not a problem.

Broadmoor is set in some of the most beautiful countryside you have ever seen. The hospital itself is huge. It is set in 416 acres in all, including 53 acres within the security perimeter, and is completely surrounded by pine forest.

Every Monday morning at 9.00am on the dot, a siren is tested. It's loud — very loud. It sounds like a war-time air-raid siren. If the siren goes off at any other time, it lets the nearby sleepy village of Crowthorne know that some dangerous patient has escaped. A blood-curdling warning.

Deep inside Broadmoor there is a heated swimming pool. Sometimes on a visit, if it was a hot day, we were allowed to sit on the terrace. If the wind was blowing in the right direction, you could sometimes catch the squeals of the inmates while they frolicked in the pool.

Ron never swam in the pool. He would never have taken a dip with all the nutters.

In the main hall, theatre companies visit once a month and put on some spectacular shows for the patients. Again, Ron never attended not wanting to socialise with the inmates. Saturday night dances were a regular occurrence and one of the only times that males and females were allowed to mix. Ron never went, saying that he didn't want to dance with the mad people.

Imagine all the nutters getting together to have a dance. I would like to have been a fly on the wall. Saturday night fever — can you imagine it?

Ron was in Broadmoor from 25 July 1979 until his death on 17 March 1995. Sixteen long years.

2

Gun in Loft

Ron and I were married for five years but, even though he's gone now, I still feel his presence almost every day of my life — I married a Kray and I will always be a Kray.

Of course, I have many mementoes of our time together, including a suitcase stuffed full of letters. Some are trivial, some are business, some divulge secrets of an unsolved murder and unanswered questions. Then there are the wedding photos, and the cards from the many bouquets he always sent me.

After he died in 1995, I inherited nothing, despite being named as a beneficiary in his will. I didn't mind that; I had had my time with Ron and no one could take that away from me.

But then I discovered that Ron *had* left me something, something I wanted nothing to do with — the gun he used to shoot George Cornell in The Blind Beggar pub in 1966.

The story of the gun started while Ron was still

alive and I was on an ordinary everyday visit, sitting at the same old Formica table in Broadmoor's visiting hall.

Ron wanted me to meet up with a friend and bring the man to visit him — nothing unusual about that, I was always picking people up and taking them on visits. I asked Ron, 'How will I recognise him?'

Ron smiled. 'You just will,' and he was right.

Later that week, I pulled up at Maidstone station, stopped the car and parked it in a bay in front of the flower stall. Just at that moment, the heavens seemed to open up and it started to rain. I couldn't believe it. Just my bloody luck. Hurriedly, I fumbled to lock my car door, all the time trying to keep my umbrella over my head to keep my hair dry.

But it was too late; it was soaking wet and already starting to frizz. I half ran towards the station entrance, my eyes scanning all the different people scurrying in and out of the station like ants. I noticed a young girl snogging a boy with a rucksack on his back; they didn't seem to notice the pouring rain. There was an old lady wearing a plastic mac fumbling to put up her umbrella before she stepped out into the rain.

Where the fuck is he? Then I spotted him. He was standing on the corner sheltering from the rain, the collar of his cashmere overcoat turned up to guard against the chill winds. There he was, the 'Cat Man'. In the 1950s and 1960s, he was one of the best cat burglars in London, but he hadn't earned his nickname because of that — it was for the simple reason that he liked cats.

Ron was right; I did recognise him straight away. His real name was Charlie Clark and he was every bit the gangster. I suppose he was smaller than I expected. But he stood tall — tall and proud.

He was, of course, 'suited and booted' in a well-cut, pin-striped suit and a cashmere overcoat draped around his shoulders, smelling slightly of moth balls. As I approached, he growled, 'You must be The Colonel's wife.'

He held my hand tightly and gave me the customary kiss on the cheek. As we headed back towards my car, Charlie lagged behind. He seemed to be walking with a slight limp, but I didn't take much notice at the time. We started chatting about trivial things like the weather. He was a nice enough man, as were most of Ron's friends.

But I wasn't looking forward to the long journey to Broadmoor. I knew I had at least a couple of hours' drive ahead of me, and I was going to have to listen to the same old waffle. I'd heard it all a million times before.

'I remember when ... blah ... blah ... blah ...'

But it didn't matter how many times I'd heard it, I couldn't be rude, I had to pretend it was the first time. I knew the Cat Man hadn't seen Ron for over 25 years and he wanted to tell me all about his involvement with Reg and Ron — from beginning to end. And God did he drone on.

As we dropped down on to the M25 on our long journey to Crowthorne in Berkshire, I really wanted to turn the radio on or slip my favourite tape into the cassette player, but I couldn't because the Cat Man wanted to tell me all about Ron.

He wanted to tell me every little detail, three times over. He told me that Ron often went to Chingford to see him and his wife Sylvia at their bungalow. He sometimes used the bungalow for the odd 'business meeting', and it was also used as a hide-out when one of the Firm was in trouble and needed a safe place. He chatted on and on. All I wanted to do was get through the bloody traffic. I knew Ron would be waiting. He hated it if anyone was late for a visit. I could understand that in one way. All Ron had to do was get up in the morning, shower and shave, then wait for his visitor to arrive.

The visitor, on the other hand, usually had to run the gauntlet of the M25. Never in his wildest imagination could Ron have imagined there being that much traffic on the road. On the odd occasion that I was late, I would feebly try to explain about the traffic, but it was just inconceivable to him. I used to tease him and say that the last time he was out, hansom cabs were still being used. He would laugh, but he'd still have the needle that I was late. By the time Charlie and I reached Broadmoor, I was really anxious. I screeched the car into the car park almost on two wheels. We were half-an-hour late, but Charlie wouldn't be rushed.

It seemed to take forever for him to limp into the reception area. Thank God it had stopped raining. At least my hair wouldn't frizz any more.

Getting into Broadmoor is very difficult. Every visitor has their own ID card and you can only get that if you are on the patient's visitors list. To get permission to visit, you have to be approved by the Home Office.

Once you've been issued with your card, the computer system takes over. Your ID card has got a bar code similar to the ones used in a supermarket. It's quite simple; you hand your card to one of the nurses in the reception area and they run it through a swipe machine, just like a credit card. It is virtually impossible to duplicate because a picture of your face comes up on the computer, so there is no doubt about who you are. The system is designed to be foolproof, which is just as well when you think of the high-security prisoners that are held in Broadmoor.

Charlie was a first time visitor, so the officer had to issue him with a new card and that meant he had to have his photograph taken. It's all done automatically. You have to stand on two plastic footprints in front of a video recorder and look up. The picture is then automatically put on to an ID card. After that you go through all the security checks. First, the metal detectors. You have to put your handbag on to a small tray on the side of the machine before you walk through. If you are wearing a belt or anything metal, you have to remove it. Charlie and I went through OK. But Charlie seemed a bit wary of it all. I think it was the next bit he was worried about — being searched. I don't think he liked the idea of that at all. Usually, the female officers deal with the women and the male officers deal with the men. Sometimes it is the other way round but the male officers are not allowed to touch you so they use a metal detector all over your body. They run their fingers down the collar of your jacket and round the cuffs and if you have turn-ups on your trousers they search there, too.

They also look into your ears and up your nose, in case somebody is stupid enough to try and smuggle drugs into the hospital. Once you have been cleared, you are ushered through automatic doors.

The doors on the other side don't open until the other ones are closed behind you, so you are enclosed in a glass bubble with the officers all around you.

It can feel quite claustrophobic and a bit frightening. Once the glass doors are opened, you start the long walk to the visiting hall. It's an unreal kind of a walk, not a pleasant one. It's now that you realise that you are in the confines of Broadmoor, the maximum security hospital for the criminally insane.

The first thing that strikes you is the high brick walls surrounding you. In parts, they are topped with barbed wire. The old Victorian building looked bleak, but the grounds are huge and beautifully landscaped. The burly officers escort you along the narrow pathways and occasionally they shout out at you to stop. That's when a party of inmates is coming in the opposite direction. At no time can the two parties mingle, in case one of the inmates tries to pass himself off as a visitor and escape. But that could never happen. The guards are far too aware of that. All patients and visitors are counted and double-checked at each gate and only then is the order given by walky-talky to open each gate. In addition to all this, every movement inside and surrounding Broadmoor, is monitored by CCTV (closed-circuit television).

As Charlie and I approached the visiting hall, he was blissfully unaware of all the security. He was far too excited about seeing Ron after all this time. I was making all the right noises at the right times — at least I think I was. Then I heard a clatter behind me. At first I didn't take any notice.

Then I looked at Charlie and saw that he was hopping. I couldn't make out what was going on until one of the officers shouted, ' 'E're, Kate, I think you've dropped something!'

As I looked around, there was a leg lying on the pavement and Charlie was hopping about with his trouser-leg flapping in the wind.

The plastic leg had a sock and a shoe on it and attached to the end was a tie, just an ordinary paisley neck-tie. I didn't really know what to do. For a moment, I was embarrassed — not for me, but for poor old Charlie. I ran back to the pink plastic leg, picked it up and put it under my arm. Charlie wasn't flustered.

'That's my leg,' he said. 'Give me a hand, Kate!'

He put his arm around my shoulder and hopped the rest of the way to the visitors' hall. It was so bizarre and comical, just like having a kangaroo beside me. On enetering the hall, you have to stop at one point, which left Charlie hopping on the spot. At the time, all I could think was, 'Oh my God, what will Ron make of it all?'

By now, we had actually got into the main building. Charlie hopped up the main corridor into the big assembly hall. There was another line of patients walking past us, giving us blank looks. It must have seemed strange, a one-legged man hopping about and a funny-looking blond bird with a false leg under her arm. The officers must have wondered who the patients were — us or them.

The visiting area looks like a big school assembly hall. On one side, it has a raised stage with faded blue velvet curtains. There are tea-stained Formica tables, each surrounded by four chairs. Sometimes, the patients are waiting for their visitors and sometimes you have to wait for the inmates to be escorted over. This particular day, as we walked into the hall, Ron was waiting for us. When he saw me, he stood up.

He looked stunning, in a Prince of Wales checked cashmere suit, with a red silk tie and a red silk hankie, and a beautiful, white starched shirt — double-cuffed, of course. He was wearing his best pair of tortoiseshell glasses.

He looked as if he had just stepped off a cruise liner.

I walked towards him with the false leg under my arm and this chap hopping about beside me — Ron howled with laughter and hugged me.

I threw my hands up in the air and laughed, trying to explain. 'His leg fell off as we walked across the yard.'

Ron, being forever the gentleman, whispered, 'Put it under the table, Kate, and say no more about it.'

So I slid the false leg under the table as discreetly as I could. Once we got the niceties out of the way, we sat down. I sat on Ron's left side because he was deaf in his left ear, and Charlie sat on the right so Ron could hear what he said. That way, even if Ron missed anything, I could fill him in later. That was the way it had always been, ever since I first met Ron.

The skinny waiter arrived at our table to take our order. They are not ordinary waiters at Broadmoor — they are inmates who have committed some heinous crime or another. Staff call them trustees, and issue them with little red storemen's jackets. They all seemed nice enough lads. But I did used to wonder what they had done to be in Broadmoor. Sometimes I would ask Ron and he would tell me.

There was one occasion when Ron had a stiff neck. I told him he should get someone to give him a massage. On the next visit, I asked Ron how his neck was.

'Yeah, Kate, you were right, a massage did work.'

I asked him who had given him the massage. Ron pointed to a tall, willowy man sitting at another table.

'That's him over there,' he said.

I asked Ron what he was in for. Ron's face was expressionless.

'He strangled his entire family.'

'And you let him ...' I stuttered, 'and you let him ... massage your fucking neck! Are you mad?'

Ron howled with laughter. 'Yeah ... I am mad — I'm in Broadmoor.'

Ron always treated the waiters by buying them cigarettes and sweets. Patients are not allowed to handle money, so when they wanted refreshments they have to put it on what is called a 'rec'. The waiter came over and asked Ron what he would like. Ron asked Charlie. 'Tea, coffee or lager?' Charlie said he would have a beer, the same as Ron — Kaliber, non-alcoholic. I had a pot of tea. The waiter went off and came back a little bit later with the chilled beers and carefully put them down on the tea-stained table. Ron took the pad and pen and signed for our drinks. As usual, he wouldn't allow anybody else to pay.

The conversation started to pick up. I wasn't particularly interested in what they were on about because it was all before my time. I have been on a million of these visits, and they are all basically the same. But I had to give them the impression I was interested.

You know the sort of thing. I made all the right noises but without really taking in what was being said. I knew it was the first time that Charlie had seen Ron for such a long time and it would have been rude of me not to have shown some interest. After visits, I used to tease Ron by saying, 'It's like a couple of old soldiers talking about the war.'

He used to laugh and thought it was funny but, at the same time, I had to show a bit of respect. So there were Charlie and Ron chatting away about the old days. After about 45 minutes of trivia, Ron would get bored. I knew that few people could keep his attention for longer than an hour. He just lost concentration. This wasn't a reflection on the person visiting him, it was just the way Ron was.

I looked at my watch. I knew it would soon be the time when Ron would say, 'I am going to ask you to leave now. No offence, but I want to speak to my wife alone.'

But on this particular occasion, before he ended the visit, Ron leaned over and whispered something to Charlie. He then looked at me and in a secret, furtive sort of way, whispered, 'Kate, Charlie is going to give you a box ... a special box.'

There wasn't anything unusual in that. I used to have hundreds of boxes delivered to me. They generally contained Ron's personal possessions, like old photos and knick-knacks. I used to store them in my loft.

You have to remember that the twins had been away for a long time. Most of their personal effects are scattered about all over the country with friends. After Ron and I married, one of the things he started doing was to pull in all his possessions and give them to me to look after. That way, he knew where they all were.

I often used to pick up a box here or a package there, so when he told me about the tea-chest from old Charlie, I just said, 'OK.'

Charlie stood up and I helped him to retrieve his false leg from under the table. He looked at Ron and his eyes filled with tears. He knew he would never see him again. It was quite emotional as they hugged each other for the last time. Eventually he was ready to leave. He put his arm around my shoulder and hopped to the end of the visiting hall. I handed him and his leg over to one of the officers like a old parcel. They took him back to the main reception. I

went back to Ron and he smiled. I shook my head.
Ron certainly did know some colourful characters.
He leaned over, took my hand and whispered, 'Don't
tell anyone about the box. Pick it up, don't look
inside until I say, and hide it somewhere safe.'

Ronnie knew he could trust me. He was sure I
wouldn't open the box until he said it was OK.

But I've got to hold my hands up and admit that
curiosity had got the better of me in the past. I had
peeked a look in other boxes, but there was nothing
particularly interesting, just personal effects of Ron's
that he wanted me to look after.

What people don't understand is that Ron had no
family on the outside, just friends, which is why all
his possessions were stored with different people.

A box here a box there. After so many years in
prison, it is hard to keep track of who's got what. I
didn't mind storing them in my loft. What I didn't
realise was that there was so bloody much of it.

Before I knew it, I was up to my ears in boxes.
After the first half-dozen I never even bothered
looking inside them any more, I just pugged them
up somewhere safe and Ron was just glad he knew
where they all were.

The visit with old Charlie Clark had gone well.
Ron and I had a laugh about his leg falling off — he
thought it was really amusing. He laughed and said,
'That will make a good story for a book, Kate. You
will have to remember that one.'

We finished our visit and I went back out to
Charlie, who, by this time, had tied his leg back on
and was waiting patiently in the reception. When we
got outside Broadmoor, he broke down and cried. He
couldn't believe how well Ron had looked. He never
said much after that, he was quiet all the way home.
It may sound silly, but it was as if he felt he could

now die in peace. Maybe that sounds dramatic, but I honestly got that feeling from him. And perhaps it wasn't so dramatic after all because, by a strange twist of fate, a few months later Charlie was brutally murdered. This time, it was definitely nothing to do with the Krays!

When Charlie and I eventually pulled into the station, I said my goodbyes to the old man and I remember thinking at the time how old he suddenly looked. I shuddered. I watched him disappear on to the platform.

I never thought that that would be the last time I would see him. I got back into my car and forgot all about Charlie Clark and the bloody old tea-chest.

A week went by before I received a phonecall from him saying he had got the box out of storage. 'Oh shit!' I thought; now I had to arrange for someone to pick the bloody thing up. So I phoned a friend called Razor. He would do anything for the twins. I explained that I wanted him to go to Dover for me and pick up the tea-chest. He was more than happy to oblige.

'Leave it to me, Kate. I'm on my way.'

A couple of hours later, he knocked on my door.

'One tea-chest — present and correct,' he joked and plonked the ancient wooden chest down on my lilac carpet. It was covered in old ink stamps and torn labels hung off the side. The top of it had been nailed firmly down.

'It's heavy!' Razor warned.

Between us, we struggled to get the chest into the loft along with the other dusty old boxes. Eventually we made it, and there it stayed for the next 6 years.

Once I took possession of the box, I didn't hear much of Charlie Clark. I did receive a couple of letters from him, but they didn't say much, just how pleased he was to meet me, and how nice it was to see Ron again. Oh yeah, and how he had written to Margaret Thatcher, and demanded that the Twins be released! He was spearheading a campaign to set them free. He was a funny old boy, but one thing was certain — he loved Ron, and would have done anything for him.

Nearly a year later, I was sitting on the sofa at home eating egg and chips off a tray on my lap, watching the early evening news on the TV, when the newsreader announced that a man had been brutally murdered in Dover. Then a picture of a man opening a front door was shown. It was only on the screen for a few seconds. I was sure it looked like Charlie.

I phoned the TV station straight away and asked for more information. They confirmed it was him. I was shocked.

They explained that a young lad called Shane Keeler had broken into Charlie's flat. He was high on drugs and looking for money for a fix. Charlie had confronted him. Even as frail as he was, and with only one leg, he put up a brave fight. Shane Keeler beat and stabbed Charlie beyond recognition. What a terrible way to die.

I remember on that long journey to Broadmoor that rainy day, Charlie shaking his head in disbelief as he told me about some yobs who had teased him in a pub. He explained that he was sitting in the corner enjoying a quiet pint when one of the thugs approached him and knocked off his cap. When Charlie stood up to take them on, they roared with laughter and jeered, 'Sit down, Granddad.'

Charlie mumbled, 'You can't talk to me like that. I used to be somebody.'

It's sad. Getting old really hits tough guys hard.

I've seen it happen with many of Ron's friends. It breaks them. It was a terrible way for Charlie to die. But he was brave to the end. At least he had a go. Shane Keeler was only 19 years old. Charlie never stood a chance. There is a well-known saying that if you live by the sword, you die by the sword. That's true of Charlie. He was a gangster and died a gangster's death — violently.

As usual, I phoned Ron at 8.00pm that night and said, 'I've got some bad news for you. Charlie Clark's dead. He has been beaten to death.'

Ron was a bit quiet, and told me to visit him the next day.

Early the next morning, I drove to Broadmoor to give him the details. I explained all about it but Ron couldn't take it in — I had to tell him three times over. I thought Ron would be livid with the boy. Maybe, I thought, he would arrange for somebody to give the lad a slap when he was put inside. But he didn't. He just thought the whole thing was sad. It was sad what had happened to Charlie.

But it was even sadder that a young boy had ruined his life. I suppose Ron knew what the boy had to look forward to for the rest of his life. To be locked away for a very long time in some of the toughest prisons in the country. Ron also knew that the boy would often wish that it was him who had died. So Ron wasn't angry, he was just sad.

We found out when Charlie was going to be buried and Ron sent a big wreath from him and Reg. He also kept tabs on Shane Keeler's trial. I had to get the local newspapers so he could read how long his sentence would be. After Ron read that he got life, he felt sad about the whole business. To be honest, I then forgot about Charlie Clark until, that is, I came across the dusty old tea-chest hidden in the loft.

I hadn't given it a thought. But three months after Ronnie's death, I broke a couple of floor tiles in my kitchen and I needed to replace them. I knew there were a couple in the loft, so I decided to go up and have a look. I got the old aluminium ladder, put it up to the hatch and climbed up with a torch. I hated going into the loft because I loathe spiders, but I knew I couldn't avoid it this time.

Slowly, I shone the torch around in the darkness. I couldn't see much, just odds and ends — a broken lamp shade, an old Christmas tree. And, of course, Ron's boxes. I had forgotten all about them. But there in the corner, covered in cobwebs, was the old tea-chest. Once I had spotted it, curiosity got the better of me. I heaved myself up into the damp darkness, being careful to walk only on the rafters. As I edged my way towards the tea-chest I felt something lightly fall on to my face. In blind panic, I squealed. Quickly, I brushed my forehead hoping it wasn't a spider, but it was just a cobweb.

The tea-chest was filthy. I started dragging it across the rafters. Once I reached the hatch, I wasn't sure how I was going to climb down the ladder and hold the chest at the same time. I put my feet firmly on the rungs of the ladder and balanced the tea-chest on my head. The chest didn't feel very heavy, it was more awkward than anything else.

Once I had got it to the bottom of the ladder, I couldn't wait to open it. First, I shook it. I tried to pull the top off but it was nailed firmly down so I couldn't budge it. So I had to get a screwdriver from the kitchen drawer and lever it off. As the lid was slowly worked loose, it creaked and a musty scent wafted from the inside of the box. It smelled a bit like an old damp church. The lid fell to the floor with a loud bang, and a small spider ran across the top. I jumped back in fright as the noise seemed to echo across the landing. I peered inside — it was only half full. At that moment, the light flickered in the hallway. For a second, I froze. I remembered what Ron had said, that I was not to look inside the box until he told me. Maybe the lights flickering was Ron's way of telling me not to go any further! It was quite eerie to think that Ron was the last person who had had his hands in the box.

I went back to the box and looked inside. There were just bits and pieces, odds and ends, things that obviously meant something to Ron. There was a white cotton shirt. I knew it was Ron's because it had a seventeen-and-a-half-inch neck, and it had the initials RK beautifully embroidered on the pocket.

Wrapped in some faded, crumpled tissue paper were some superb 18-carat gold cuff-links, 1960s' style, with Ron's initials set in diamonds. There was also a big bundle of old paper money which really stank.

I reached inside the box and lifted the bundle out, but as I did so, the rotting elastic band that was holding the money together snapped, sending the old ten bob and five pound notes flying everywhere. Frantically, I scooped them up in a pile beside the chest. There were also lots of old pictures and photographs of Reg and Ron with famous celebrities.

As I went through the box, I felt a bit sad that Ron wasn't with me. Some of the things made me smile, like the slight tide mark around the collar of his shirt. I held it to my face and smelt it, imagining that I could still smell Ron's aftershave. All the feelings I had for Ron came flooding back. Carefully, I hung the shirt over the banisters. The box was now empty.

The bottom was lined with an old 1960s newspaper, the headlines screaming about the Swinging Sixties and the Beatles, their every move being documented. I thumbed through the papers. Isn't it funny how an old newspaper can draw your attention away from something as interesting as the mysterious contents of the box. Riveting reading, but back to the chest.

I divided the bits and pieces into little piles; things I wanted to keep and things to throw away. I looked down at my hands; they were black. I decided to throw the tea-chest away. I started to bump it down the stairs. As I did, I heard a thump. It seemed to come from the bottom of the chest. I couldn't make out what it was; I thought the chest was empty. When I got to the bottom of the stairs, I picked the tea-chest up and shook it. There seemed to be something still inside.

I couldn't understand it. I picked up the screwdriver, reached inside the chest and stabbed the bottom. To my amazement, the screwdriver made a hole. I couldn't believe there was a false bottom. Inside, I saw a bright yellow, fluffy cloth, the sort your granny used as a duster. As I picked it up and unwrapped it, there, lying in my hand, was an old gun. A 9mm Mauser Automatic.

I was stunned. I remember reading that the gun that had killed George Cornell in the 1960s was a 9mm Mauser Automatic. At that moment I didn't know what to do, so I smelt the barrel. I don't know why — I must have watched too many cowboy films. I don't know what I expected to smell — smoke, maybe. Then I smiled to myself.

It was just like Ron. Even though he was dead, he still had an air of mystery surrounding him. I don't think he particularly wanted me to have the gun.

Maybe he just forgot it was there. But I don't think so. I think he just wanted to know where it was. Now I had it. I didn't know what to do with it. I had never discussed with Ron what he did with the gun after he shot Cornell. It was a taboo subject.

When I was with Ron, there were always lots of other things to talk about and never enough time to cover everything. Just everyday things, like Ron asking me to buy him new vests or socks, or to pick up or drop off various packages.

Sometimes on a visit, he would tell me things about the past and I didn't hide the fact that I made a mental note of them. He knew that what he had to say was explosive. He wasn't a fool — he was a very shrewd man. He use to tease me and say, 'One day, when I'm dead, you will have to write a book of all these stories.' Never a truer word spoken.

How inconceivable. There I was, holding the gun that had killed George Cornell, the gun that had eluded the police for decades.

I wrapped it back up in the grubby duster and dragged the old tea chest out into my back garden for the dustmen to take away. I went back inside and phoned Ron's friend, Razor. I laughed to myself and wondered how I was going to tell him. I didn't think it was wise to tell him something like that over the phone. I thought it best to ask him to come over. He took ages to answer and when he finally did, he sounded a bit grumpy.

'Razor,' I whispered, 'I think you had better come over, I have got something to show you.' At first he was reluctant to come before lunchtime. Sensing the urgency in my voice, he eventually agreed.

I didn't know what to do while I waited for Razor to come round. I tried reading a magazine, then I turned on the TV. But it was no good, I couldn't concentrate on anything. I wandered around my living-room clutching the gun still wrapped in the yellow duster. I decided to make myself a nice cup of tea. I cut myself a huge slice of chocolate cake. After one bite I put it down; I just could not face it.

The only thing I could think of was what the hell was I going to do with the bloody gun. 'I know,' I thought, 'I'll put it in my cutlery drawer along with the knives and forks.'

About an hour later, there was a loud knock at the door. I opened it and looked at Razor. His eyes were still half closed.

'It'd better be good,' he yawned.

As I pulled the blackened gun from the cutlery drawer I smirked to myself. Oh, it's good all right!

I handed him the weapon. He looked puzzled. Then he laughed.

'Where did you get this from?'

I explained all about Charlie Clark and the old tea-chest. I told him that it was the gun Ron had used to kill George Cornell. I was positive about it.

'I think you are right, but what the fuck do you want me to do with it?' he asked.

At that precise moment, I really didn't know. But one thing I was sure of was that I wanted it out of the house. You can bet your life it wasn't deactivated and as I didn't have a gun licence, not to mention the effect of my name, it wouldn't have looked too good if the Old Bill had wanted to give me a spin. I just needed time to think. Razor took the gun for safe-keeping until I could decide what to do with it.

A few days later I collected the gun, still wrapped in the yellow duster. I took it to another friend of Ron's who deactivated it for me, as there was no way I wanted to be nicked for possession.

Word spread like wildfire that I had the gun — the gun that killed Cornell — everybody wanted it. But Ron had left the gun to me and I felt that it was my duty to decide what to do with it. I wasn't sure. One day I would decide to keep the gun, the next day I was positive I was going to throw it in the river. I even walked down to the river and stood on the bridge toying with the gun. I wanted to throw it in, I knew it was the best thing to do, but I couldn't do it.

Images came flooding back of Ron walking into The Blind Beggar Pub and blowing George Cornell's brains all over the carpet. I couldn't do it, I couldn't throw it away. I wrapped it back up in the duster and went home.

The next day, I phoned my bank and made an appointment to see the Manager to discuss the arrangements for a safety deposit box. So I pay the premium each month to an undisclosed bank where the gun is kept until such time as I can decide what to do with it.

Ronnie loved guns; he was strangely fascinated by them. I remember a time when I went to see him in Broadmoor. I had a lighter in the shape of a Derringer gun. It was only tiny, with an inlaid mother-of-pearl handle. I thought I would have a little game with him when he lit up a fag. I waited until he had poured out a can of beer, then, as usual, he took a cigarette from the packet. Knowing that the patients are not allowed to have matches, I rummaged about in my bag to find the little gun. I put my finger on the trigger and, in a flash, I held the gun to his head. With Ron, you never knew how he was going to take things. Sometimes he would be OK and sometimes he would turn a bit funny.

It wasn't anything he said, just the look in his

eyes. On this particular day, I put the gun to his head and said, 'Freeze, or I'll blow your brains out.'

Ron sat there, not moving a muscle. He didn't turn his head to the side, he didn't jump, he just sat there. He just froze on the spot. He simply moved his eyes to look at me.

I pulled the trigger. CLICK. A little tiny flame popped out the end. He turned his head and glared at me. He held my gaze with a thunderous look in his eyes. In a flash, his face softened and he howled with laughter; he just could not stop laughing. He snatched the lighter out of my hand and, still laughing, said, 'You've got to do it, Kate. Go down to the end where all the officers sit and tell them you are taking me hostage. Go on, I dare you.'

I squinted my eyes, pursed my lips and, with a twinkle in my eye, I squealed, 'All right then, I will.'

We strolled down towards the officers pretending we were going to the shop. Ron's hands were deep in his pockets and his face gave nothing away. The gun was half hidden up my sleeve and I tried very hard not to giggle..

As we approached the officers, a couple of them looked up. They didn't take much notice of us, they were more interested in their half-eaten sandwiches and drinking tea. I pulled the gun out and I shouted, 'He's coming with me, I'm taking him out of here.'

They didn't raise an eyebrow.

'Pack it up Kate,' they scoffed, 'and stop mucking about.'

'I'm not mucking about,' I replied, 'I'm deadly serious.'

They all started laughing and waved me back to my table.

Ron was now howling with laughter again. He went to the toilet, and I went back to our table and stuffed the gun back into my handbag. No one made any fuss, it was just one big laugh. When Ron eventually came back, he asked if anyone had said anything. I said, 'No, they all thought it was funny.'

Ron laughed and said, 'Imagine that getting in the *News of the World*, I can just see the headlines now: KRAY TAKEN HOSTAGE AT GUNPOINT.'

*   *   *

Lots of things have been said about Ron. What a bad temper he had. How he could change so quickly. How you never knew where you were with him. To a certain degree, that was true. Like I said, you could always tell by the look in his eyes what sort of mood he was in. I could always tell straight away if he was in a good mood. I saw him happy and sad, I saw him cry and I saw him bloody mad. But I never saw him be violent towards anybody.

He would tell me everything if I asked him. Like the time he tied a man called Lennie Hamilton to a chair, and then branded him across each cheek with a red-hot poker all because he had shown disrespect to a woman. He told me about a boxer who had walked into a pub and took a right liberty with Ron, taunting him by saying, 'You've put on a bit of weight, ain't ya?'

Ron went mad; you couldn't say things like that to Ron and get away with it. He followed the boxer out to the toilets. Ten minutes later, they found Joe, the boxer, with half his face on the floor. He needed 70 stitches.

I don't think these were whimsical acts of violence by Ron, or even dishing out a punishment. But one thing you could not do with Ron was to take a liberty.

Ronnie Fields, another one of Ron's friends, who has just received a ten-year stretch for the biggest drug's haul ever, told me about when they were in Parkhurst together. Ron was sitting at a table eating his dinner from one of those little tin trays. He was surrounded by his friends when one of them said to him, 'Eat your greens up, Ron, it'll make your hair curl.'

In a flash, Ron turned. Once again, someone had taken a liberty. A silence fell across the dinner table. Everybody knew that Ron had taken it the wrong way.

He picked up his metal tray and smashed it across the bloke's nose. Blood squirted everywhere, and the tip of his nose rolled across the dirty floor amongst the fag ends.

Everyone knew that Ron was unpredictable and how dangerous it was if he was in one of his menacing moods. If you were unlucky enough to cross him, or he took a dislike to you, you would inevitably pay a price. That's what happened to Peter Sutcliffe, otherwise known as the Yorkshire Ripper.

'Get the Yorkshire Ripper,' Ron hissed. 'I don't care how, but I want him done. Mark him for life.'

That was the order Ron gave in 1983 when he decided that it was time the Ripper paid his dues for killing 13 women from 1975 to 1980, by clubbing his helpless victims on the back of their heads with a hammer. He had violated the criminal's code of honour, according to Ron, by killing women, and in Ron's own words, 'That was right out of order.'

He put the word out that it was time the Ripper paid. It soon passed along the grapevine and, within days, news reached Parkhurst. It eventually reached the ears of an inmate called Jimmy Costello who was serving ten years for firearms offences. The Ripper was also there, unaware that his face was shortly to be ripped to bits.

It took just over a week from Ron's initial comments about Sutcliffe, for Glaswegian Costello to slash him across the cheek, eye and neck with a broken coffee jar. Sutcliffe needed 30 stitches in his face. When Ron heard, he sat back, smiled and thought it a job well done.

That was in 1983. It's weird, really, because a little while after that, Sutcliffe was moved to Broadmoor and put in the very next cell to Ron. But they never spoke.

Often, when Ron was on a visit, Sutcliffe would also have visitors because they were both known as 'high-profile' prisoners and would be monitored more closely than some of the others.

I would go into the visiting hall to find both Ron and Sutcliffe. I remember one hot summer's day, I was wearing a really short dress, showing my bare legs. As I walked across the hall, I had to pass the Ripper. He was staring at me so intently it was as though he was transfixed. It made me feel sick. I said to Ron, 'Did you see the way he was looking at me? It was horrible.'

Ron didn't bat an eyelid. 'Don't worry about that, just sit yourself down. See those scars on his face? I sorted him a long time ago. A mate of mine did that with a coffee jar.'

Ron whispered and told me that his friend, Jimmy Costello, had got an extra five years on his sentence for attacking Sutcliffe with the coffee jar.

But Ron was still annoyed that he had dared to look at me. He must have had a word with him because, from that day on, Sutcliffe never looked my way again.

Ron lived by the sword — sometimes literally — and, if necessary, he would have been prepared to die by it. After I had seen the Kray film, I asked, 'You didn't do all those horrible things, did you, Ron?'

His face was cold and expressionless. 'Yeah, I did, and a lot worse than that,' he whispered.

I can't say he scared me, because I always knew I was safe with Ron but, as I said before, you never knew which way he was going to go. And he was never remorseful about anything he had done. He was a criminal and he was proud of it.

That's why Ron was not interested in writing books and poetry like Reg. Ron did write poetry from time to time, but he once told me, 'I will always be known as Ronnie Kray, murderer. Not Ronnie Kray, the poet.'

3

Warts and All

HOMOSEXUAL USED SEX TO BLACKMAIL HIS VIP CHUMS screamed the newspaper headlines in 1964.

Now, in 1997, nothing has changed! Only today in the Sunday newspapers, the headlines screamed again: TORY MP CONFESSES TO HOMOSEXUAL AFFAIR.

More than 30 years on, the media is still obsessed with MPs and their sex lives.

In the 1960s, Lord Boothby MP took *The Mirror* newspaper to court over his alleged affair with Ron. At the time, there was a national outcry. Afraid of saying goodbye to his political career, Boothby strenuously denied the allegations. Palms were greased in the highest circles, money changed hands at an alarming rate, and the result was that Boothby was awarded £40,000 for libel.

Obviously, I would have been far too young to remember anything about the Press stories, but the majority of the time Ron liked to talk about the old days — after all, they were all he had left. The life he had in Broadmoor was just an existence, although he always tried to make the best of it; nothing really happened, every day was the same. He was eager to tell me about his life on the outside when he had been free. Of course, there were times when he didn't want to talk, and then he'd snap at me that it 'was all in the past'. But, for some reason, one day on a visit, Ron was adamant that he wanted to tell me all about a man called Leslie Holt.

Normally, when Ron talked about the past it was usually because something had jogged his memory — and what a memory he had. It was sharp as a razor, despite his illness. As he talked, it was as if in his mind he'd gone back to those days. He could remember every detail.

This particular day, something had come up in the newspaper about Lord Boothby, so Boothby was on Ron's mind when I visited him.

As soon as he walked into the visiting hall, I sensed he was in a foul mood. It was the look on his face. Someone was in for it — hopefully not me. When Ron was gunning for someone he called them 'slags and rats' and on this visit there were quite a few 'slags and rats' being thrown about.

For a change, it was not me who had upset him. All of Ron's real friends have, at one time or another, been a 'slag and a rat'. Me included. Indeed, you weren't anyone to Ronnie Kray unless he had called you that. This particular day it was Boothby's turn, and it didn't matter that he had been a Lord. To Ron, he was still a 'slag and a rat'.

Ron didn't differentiate between a dustman and a Lord. To him, they were all the same — potential earners.

I gave Ron his fags and fumbled in my bag for a

light. As I struck the match to light his cigarette, out of the corner of his mouth he exhaled, sighed, lent back in his chair and continued on about Boothby.

He laughed and said that Boothby was a kinky Lord and had had lots of boyfriends, the younger the better. Ron stood up. I thought he was going to the toilet but instead he produced from his pocket a black-and-white photograph. He pointed at a fat old man sitting on a settee in what looked like a palatial apartment. Simply from the photograph, you could tell the man had class. It wasn't just his Saville Row suit that gave it away. Anyone can buy good clothes. What you cannot buy is breeding. And that's exactly what Boothby had — breeding.

'That's Lord Boothby,' Ron said, pointing at the faded print. 'And that's Leslie Holt.'

Obviously, I had heard of Lord Boothby but Leslie Holt's name didn't ring any bells with me — then again, why should it?

Ron started going on and on about Holt, insisting that he was a 'no good bastard' and that he deserved to die. He was really slagging him off. I found it hard to follow what he was saying but one thing was sure — Ron hated him.

At the end of the day, I didn't really have an opinion. I had never heard of Leslie Holt and told Ron I couldn't care less about him.

But Ron didn't listen to a word I said. He was relentless, and was determined to tell me all about him. He explained that Holt was a vain 'nancy boy' and that he was obsessed by the disfiguring warts on his hands and feet.

He was good looking, though. Good-looking enough to become one of Ronnie's boys. BINGO! For the first time, Ron had my full attention. My ears always pricked up when Ron started talking on a more personal level.

I looked at Ron as he sipped his chilled lager and gently wiped his mouth.

I winced. 'One of your boys? YUK!'

Ron laughed. 'Yeah, he was one of my boys — warts and all.'

Ron continued to say that Holt was also Lord Boothby's boyfriend. But that wasn't all. Holt wasn't satisfied with a gangster and a Lord. He involved one other person, creating a triangle with him in the middle. This other person was someone whom he thought would be useful to him, an eminent Harley Street doctor by the name of Gordon Kells, the man later charged with Leslie Holt's murder.

It seemed that the young Mr Holt had been swapped around like pass-the-parcel at a children's birthday party.

But it was no ordinary, run-of-the-mill party. Holt had champagne ideas with a brown ale pay-packet. Big ideas that needed lovers with big bank balances. He targeted high-society pals, then blackmailed them. But Holt had a problem — warts.

Being a vain man, he hated the unsightly lumps and bumps on his hands and feet and wanted them removed, whatever the cost. But he was skint and could not afford the high costs of such an operation. He was a determined man on a mission — he had to get rid of those awful warts.

It was around this time that Holt started having the affair with Dr Kells, the Harley Street doctor. Unable to afford Dr Kells' fees, Holt paid with his sexual favours. Dr Kells was due to remove the unsightly warts under a local anaesthetic, a simple operation for such an eminent surgeon, one that he had performed probably a thousand times before. But, mysteriously, Holt died.

Ron gave one of his knowing smirks. I was taken aback.

'People don't die from something like that,' I gasped.

Ron shrugged his shoulders.

I did not understand immediately what Ron was trying to tell me. His eyes narrowed. He held my arm, pulled me close and whispered, 'You silly girl, you don't really think he died from a local anaesthetic do you? The doctor was the Patsy.'

I knew what the term 'Patsy' meant — a mug who takes the blame for something — but I didn't understand what Ron meant by saying that the doctor was the 'Patsy'.

'What do you mean "he was the Patsy"?' I asked.

Ron realised he had already said more than he should. 'Oh nothing,' he snapped. 'Forget all about it.'

He had done it again. Only telling me part of the story. I became very irritable.

'Tell me more,' I insisted.

But Ron clammed up and was having none of it. I tried my best to get him to tell me more, but he wouldn't. In the seven years I was with Ron, he never brought the subject up again. But the words 'the doctor was the Patsy' has always stuck in my mind.

Now that Ron is dead and I am writing a new book, out of curiosity I decided to ask my publisher to get me the newspaper cuttings on Leslie Holt. I never expected them to tell me anything. I had a gut feeling that on that day in the visiting hall at Broadmoor, Ronnie had been trying to tell me something. But what?

The cuttings arrived on the 28 January 1997. I opened the brown envelope and briefly scanned each page — I was shocked. Leslie Holt had died mysteriously, very mysteriously, from a massive overdose of Methohexitone. It was Doctor Kells, the Harley Street surgeon, who had administered the fatal injection.

That was it. That was what Ron was trying to tell me. The doctor was the 'Patsy'. I was intrigued.

After I had finished reading all the cuttings, I smiled to myself. In his own way, Ron had led me on to something that had long been forgotten. The Old Fox. He knew I would remember what he had said. He also knew that I would find out more. He once said that nobody could get anything over on me, that I was as sharp as a tack. Well, he was right.

I don't profess to know the whole story about Leslie Holt. I will let you decide for yourselves what really happened to the vain nancy boy covered in warts.

Ron's association with Lord Boothby has been well documented, as has the libel case Boothby took out against *The Mirror* after it exposed their love affair.

Boothby always denied the affair. In those days, homosexuality was illegal for one thing, but it would have also destroyed his political career.

Ron always admitted that he was bisexual; he didn't give a damn that it was against the law — since when did breaking the law ever bother Ronnie Kray? More importantly, he loved the idea of having a relationship with a famous peer who was once Winston Churchill's Parliamentary Secretary.

While Boothby was suing the newspaper, Ron had to deny the affair. In close circles, however, he readily admitted to it as he thought it was a coup to get a Minister under his belt and, even better still, a Minister who was a Lord.

Years later Boothby found himself in court again,

denying an affair with Holt, but when Holt started to blackmail Boothby it was Ron to whom Boothby turned for help. But Leslie Holt was greedy; he was already trying to blackmail the surgeon and Boothby, but made a fatal mistake of chancing his arm, and his life, by trying to blackmail Ron over his affair with Boothby in the 1960s.

Ron was sharp and knew that his friendship with Boothby would come in handy for something. Little did he realise that his association with Boothby created waves in high places and later led to repercussions, which was the reason why both he and Reggie were made an example of with 30-year recommended prison sentences.

Lots of questions have been asked why the twins received such a long sentence for one murder each. The reason was political. Reg and Ron climbed the social ladder and mingled with royalty, MPs and Lords and Ladies, soon finding themselves way out of their depth. After the murders of Jack the Hat and George Cornell, their high-society friends became scared. Suddenly, it was no longer trendy to mingle with dangerous gangsters. They began to give The Twins a wide berth.

Whispers reverberated throughout Parliament. It was only a matter of time before faceless men in authority felt it was their duty to make an example of The Twins by giving them each a life sentence. The Judge recommended that they should each serve 30 years before they were considered for parole. At their trial in March 1969, at the Old Bailey, Mr Justice Melford Stevenson said to Ron, 'I am not going to waste words on you. The sentence is that of life imprisonment. In my view, society has earned a rest from your activities.'

For Mr Justice Melford Stevenson — known as

'The Hanging Judge' — it was the moment he had been waiting for, the climax of the longest murder trial in the history of Britain's Central Criminal Court, a high spot in his long legal career.

The Krays had stood in the dock facing their accusers for 39 days. It took the jury just six hours and fifty-four minutes to decide their guilt and, in sentencing them to life, with a recommendation of 30 years apiece, Judge Melford Stevenson was handing out the longest sentence for murder ever known at the Old Bailey.

The Government at the time hoped it would put the fear of God into any other gangster who got too big for his boots. 'It doesn't matter who you are or how big you get, we will always win' — that was the message.

Judges do not come from the East End, and they don't go to comprehensive schools. Judges and MPs often come from public schools.

The twins had the ability to attract people from all walks of life. Having power and money is one thing; Reg and Ron had plenty of that. High society has power and money, as well as the all-important breeding. If you haven't got the breeding, money and power can't buy it. You can only skirt around the edges of high society. Once you try to infiltrate it, they close ranks. Although they loved flirting with the danger that surrounded the twins, when Reg and Ron dared to cross their line they were slapped down and made an example of. And, boy, did they make an example of them.

Maybe the twins thought they were untouchable because they had lots of powerful and influential friends in high places. How wrong they were.

The newspaper headlines read: BOOTHBY AND THE GANGSTER!

Ron said that he roared with laughter when he read the paper. I asked him how the papers found out. He winked. 'Because we told them. That way, we had Boothby where we wanted him. I had to deny the affair to the world so Boothby felt he owed me a favour — and, boy, did we milk him.

Leslie Holt died in September 1979 at the age of 42, after surgery to remove a wart from his big toe. Doctor Gordon Kells was charged with manslaughter.

Leslie Holt was in his early 20s when he met Lord Boothby. He was a successful and glamorous young criminal who drove an Aston Martin, which Boothby bought for him, bearing his personalised number plates.

Although Lord Boothby always maintained that his relationship with Leslie Holt was not a sexual one, Ron insisted that it was, very much, a sexual relationship. And if anyone should have known, Ron did, because he was having a relationship with both of them.

Holt was one of six sons of a Shoreditch dustman. Lord Boothby was educated at Eton and Oxford. They made a highly unlikely couple — especially in those days — but Boothby and Holt formed a friendship that bridged the social gulf. It was so close that Holt's family and friends say that the Peer wanted to adopt the young cockney lad who was 37 years his junior. Boothby denied the gay affair, maintaining that they were just good friends, and he was quoted in the newspapers at the time, saying, 'It was a perfectly normal relationship. I met Leslie Holt at a boxing match. I took to him right away. He used to drop in a couple of times a year just for a chat. We were just good friends, and I enjoyed his company.'

Boothby went on to reveal at his posh home in Eaton Square, in London's Belgravia. 'I had no idea that Holt was a notorious crook and had been to jail several times.'

But Holt boasted to friends that it was Lord Boothby who had bought him his Aston Martin sports car. But the Peer said, 'Oh no. He bought the Aston himself.'

Why do politicians think that if they lie we will all believe them? Maybe if they lie often enough, they end up believing what they say themselves.

It was as plain as the nose on your face that Lord Boothby and Leslie Holt were gay lovers. Ron told me they were, and he should have known — he'd had affairs with both of them. Why else would Lord Boothby buy a cockney boy the most expensive car of its time. Even today, few people can afford such a luxury car — only the likes of Prince Charles and overpaid pop stars have that privilege.

Boothby was adamant and continued to deny the affair, even though Leslie Holt's mum and dad, George and Mary Holt, were taken to Lord Boothby's Eton Square house by Holt in his Aston Martin, the one that the Lord had bought for him. Holt always said that Lord Boothby was a gentleman, and was only being friendly when his parents went to his house. They sat in his beautiful apartment and drank scotch and talked for hours, but it is interesting why a man of Boothby's calibre would want to meet the local dustman. It's laughable.

Boothby also took Holt abroad and, at one time, he was Boothby's chauffeur and they travelled overseas together. He encouraged Holt's interest in the arts; he would take him to art galleries which Holt enjoyed enormously. He always said that Boothby educated him in the finer things of life. He made friends with some of London's top barristers

THIS WILL dated the 28TH SEPTEMBER One thousand nine hundred and eighty nine is made by me RONALD KRAY of Taunton Ward, Somerset House, Broadmoor Hospital, Crowthorne, Berkshire.

1. I revoke all earlier Wills.

2. This will shall not be revoked by my intended marriage to Kate Howard of 5 Forge Lane, Headcorn in the County of Kent.

3.(a) I appoint as my executor my solicitor Stephen Gerald Gold of 38 Stoke Road, Gosport in Hampshire.

(b) The said Stephen Gerald Gold may charge fees for work done by him or his Firm (whether or not the work is of a professional nature) in connection with this will and my estate on the same basis as if he were not my executor but employed to carry out the work on behalf of my executor.

4. I give to my brother Reginald Kray of H.M. Prison, Lewes in the County of Sussex all my jewellery and articles of personal use or adornment and for the avoidance of doubt these shall include my rings cross and chain and cuff links.

5. I give the rest of my estate in equal shares to such of the following as shall be living at the date of my death namely the said Kate Howard Anne Glew of 14 Mamaton Close, Priory Estate, Haywards Heath in the County of West Sussex and Charlie Smith of Taunton Ward, Somerset House, Broadmoor Hospital, Crowthorne aforesaid.

SIGNED by the Testator
in our presence and
attested by us in the
presence of the Testator
and of each other

}   *R. Kray*

CO BROADMOOR
HOSPITAL
CROWTHORNE BERKS.
CONSULTANT PSYCHIATRIST.

Ronnie Kray's will.

Opposite page:
The order of service
for Ronnie's funeral,
29 March 1995.
The service was held
at St Matthew's
Church in Bethnal
Green, and 50,000
people lined the
route from the church
to the cemetery in
Chingford.

Below: Charlie *(left)*
and Reggie *(right)*
console each other
at the funeral.
That's Alex Steen in
the background.

KATE KRAY

ST. MATTHEW'S CHURCH
BETHNAL GREEN

✝

In Loving Memory

of

RONALD KRAY

BORN 24th OCTOBER 1933
DIED 17th MARCH 1995

OFFICIATING PRIEST
FR. CHRISTOPHER BEDFORD

WEDNESDAY 29th MARCH 1995
at 12 NOON

ORDER OF SERVICE

Organ Music

OPENING SENTENCES

"MY WAY"
sung by Frank Sinatra

PRAYERS

Charlie and Reg would like to include in this Service
friends who cannot be here today, friends from Broadmoor and Prisons,
they are young Charlie, Mohammed, Joe, Paul, Bradley, Anton,
Jim, Rab, Ron, Pete, Lee, Andrew
and all others too many to mention, they are with us in spirit.

HYMN

Morning has broken,
Like the first morning,
Blackbird has spoken
Like the first bird.
Praise for the singing!
Praise for the morning!
Praise for them, springing
Fresh from the Word!

Sweet the rain's new fall
Sunlit from heaven,
Like the first dewfall
On the first grass.
Praise for the sweetness
Of the wet garden,
Sprung in completeness
Where his feet pass.

Mine is the sunlight!
Mine is the morning
Born of the one light
Eden saw play!
Praise with elation,
Praise every morning,
God's re-creation
Of the new day!

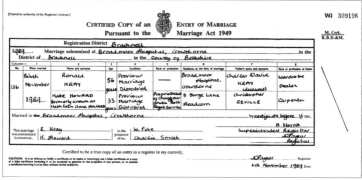

Above: Roy 'Pretty Boy' Shaw and I at the wedding reception.

Opposite page: Ronnie and I celebrate our wedding in 1989. Even in Broadmoor, Ronnie always wore suits of the finest cut!

Below: Our certificate of marriage.

Above: Ronnie, looking pensive, next to Lord Boothby. *(c Bernard Black)*.

Below: Boothby, Ronnie and Leslie Holt. Holt went under a general anaesthetic during an operation to have warts removed from his hand. He never woke up. *(c Bernard Black)*.

Reggie, Boothby and Teddy Smith – a villain who later 'disappeared'.

(c Bernard Black).

Above left: George Cornell.

Above right: Jack 'The Hat' McVitie.

Below: Ronnie, Billy Murray and friends on holiday in Barcelona during the sixties.

and had a love affair with a male executive from London's top fashion magazine.

He used to go to all the best parties and was a familiar face at London's most exclusive nightclubs.

Ron told me that Holt made no secret of being in and out of bed with many different people, and Holt told Ron that he had to put the squeeze on them to get some cash. Ron said that he had helped Holt to fence diamonds and jewels that he had stolen after having sex with his high-society friends, and that Holt was threatened on many occasions — one lover he was blackmailing threatened to have Holt's arms chopped off. But, all the time Holt was one of Ron's boys, he knew that he was safe and Ron would protect him. When he was talking to Ron, Holt just laughed and said, 'What can they do about it? Nothing.'

He had become very cocky. He had blackmailed many powerful people and upset a lot more. Another one of Holt's lovers was Dr Gordon Kells, the Harley Street surgeon, who earned himself the nickname of the 'spare parts doctor' when he began a scheme to buy kidneys and other human organs from poor overseas countries for transplant surgery in Britain. His plan was heavily criticised by other doctors, but Kells ignored his colleagues. He wrote a medical paper in which he said that the more affluent society should offer to purchase, for example, a kidney from a fit man from the Third World. If the man was offered £2,000, the doctor suggested, he would be happy because, for the cost of a kidney, he would become relatively rich in his own country.

Ron said that Leslie Holt and the surgeon became lovers shortly before Holt's untimely death. Holt decided to use the surgeon as planned, to remove his unsightly warts free of charge because, if he refused, Holt threatened to expose their relationship. Dr Kells felt unable to refuse him and the operation was booked for September 1979.

Holt arrived at Dr Kells surgery at 9.00pm on a drizzly September night. The doctor tried to turn him away.

He used every excuse possible, feebly explaining that he did not feel too well himself and that, that very day, he had been knocked down by a car and had fallen off his bike and hit his head.

Holt however, insisted that the surgery was done. He was due to have three warts removed from his feet and a cyst removed from behind his ear. Doctor Kells reluctantly agreed and gave him a local anaesthetic, but Holt complained about the pain, and was given an injection of what the doctor said was Valium.

Holt collapsed and was taken to hospital where he later died. The Police Scientific Officer, John Taylor, said that the tests revealed a massive overdose of Methohexitone, apparently 10 to 20 times higher than recommended. Pathologist Dr Ian West said that the use of the drug was totally inappropriate unless a doctor had an assistant to watch the patient's heart and breathing rate.

Strangely enough, two weeks before Holt's death, Kells' mews home was broken into and valuable antiques were stolen.

At his trial, the doctor said he did not want to treat the warts as he was feeling unwell. Mr Holt, who was returning to his home in Balenyffos, Dyfed in South Wales the following day, persuaded him to go ahead. He became very abusive and started shouting that he could not hang about. He wanted the operation done and he wanted it done now. He was determined to have his warts removed. The doctor reluctantly agreed for the sake of some peace and quiet.

Holt was 42 when he died.

In 1981, Dr Kells was eventually cleared by an Old Bailey jury of unlawful killing. Holt's story is a very strange tale. Ron obviously knew more than he was prepared to divulge. Maybe there was a cover up. I really don't know. Now that Ron, Boothby and Holt are all dead, we probably never will.

4

The Broadmoor Hilton

Ronnie Kray didn't exactly like being locked away in Broadmoor, but he made sure life was as enjoyable and comfortable as possible under the circumstances. He didn't really have a champagne and caviar lifestyle, but it wasn't far from that. Just his name, his charisma and an abundance of cash always ensured that he got what he wanted, when he wanted.

Ron never had to threaten anybody. He always told me, 'Speak nicely to people and they always do what you want.'

He must have been right because he had a network of servants inside Broadmoor, fellow inmates, ready, some even anxious, to get close to him.

I don't know if it was his name that did it or the reflected glory of being his 'friend', which perhaps gave them a greater status inside. Then again, maybe it was all the presents he bought them. But one thing is for sure; everybody seemed to want to be around

Ron, helping and doing things for him. I suppose it was their claim to fame.

For instance, Ronnie never washed or ironed his shirts, or even pressed his trousers. He always got someone else to do it for him. There was always a little band of 'helpers' or 'yes men' as I called them. I had visions of all these nutters running about saying, 'Yes, Ron ... no, Ron ... three bags full, Ron ...'

Charlie was the inmate who use to wash, starch and iron Ron's shirts. He was given a jar of coffee every week. Ron's shirts were his speciality. He took great pride in making sure that they were just how Ron liked them.

Ron changed his shirt after every visit, making 14 shirts a week. Charlie did them week in, week out, for years, for just a jar of coffee a week.

I played my part by trying to keep Ron in the style to which he had become accustomed. In the end, I found myself under arrest by the Thames Valley Police, accused of bribery and corruption. At the time, of course, I denied everything, but I have to admit now that I did pass money to a number of nurses in exchange for favours for Ron. I always paid them with a business cheque from the luxury car-hire service that I was running at the time called 'Silver Ladies'.

Ronnie wanted me to pay the officers with cash, but I said that I preferred to pay them by cheque; that way, if anything went wrong, I had evidence to prove that they had worked for me. I had to cover my arse, some way or another.

After my arrest, the police carried out a major inquiry. Broadmoor had their own internal investigation, too, resulting in two staff members being forced to quit. Only now after Ron's death can I admit that I did pay some officers large sums of money for making Ron's life easier. £500 here, £1,000 there, depending on what favour Ron had asked of them.

Some of them preferred gifts like portable televisions or microwave ovens rather than money, which drove me mad because I was the one who had to go and buy them.

Not content with just a gift, they were always so particular about what they wanted by specifying makes, models and even catalogue numbers. Sometimes I would be shopping all day in the pouring rain, trudging from shop to shop to get it right.

I remember one officer. He always insisted on electrical gifts, and once asked for a Yamaha electric organ.

He wouldn't be content with a lap-held organ, oh no, it had to be a great big free-standing one. I was expected to buy it from Dixons in Maidstone and lug it all the way to Broadmoor. Getting it there was one thing. Getting it past the security was quite a different story altogether.

Broadmoor's security is legendary — security cameras, wardens and snarling dogs. However, there was a blind spot. And guess what? Ron knew where it was!

I never used to do anything quite as dramatic as arranging secret rendezvous with 'friendly' staff at the dead of the night. It was quite simply done just before a visit. But to any passer-by it must have seemed all very cloak-and-dagger stuff, with shady-looking men loitering about in the car park talking to me out of the corner of their mouths, ready with a car boot open.

Whenever you think of furtive meetings, you always associate them with meeting under a clock at

Waterloo station, with a red carnation in your buttonhole or a copy of *The Times* under your arm.

We had our own Waterloo. The only blind spot surrounding Broadmoor was beneath the ghostly white statue of an angel deep in the grounds, in the shadow of its high walls.

To get there, you drive up the tree-lined private road towards the main building. As you approach the main doors you bear left towards the overflow car parks at the side of Broadmoor. It is there that you will find the ghostly white statue where I had my secret rendezvous.

At times, the boot of my car resembled Santa's sleigh on Christmas Eve, stuffed full of portable TVs, electric organs and microwave ovens. All that was missing was a freshly plucked turkey! I never minded ferrying stuff to and fro because I knew this enabled Ron to have what he wanted in Broadmoor, including phonecalls at one o'clock in the morning.

One night I was half asleep when the phone rang. In a daze, I reached for the receiver. On the end of the line was a gruff voice. 'Is that you, Kate? I've got a phone call for ya.'

I didn't recognise the voice. I couldn't work it out who it was. I thought it was a crank call.

'Who's this speaking?' I snapped.

'Never mind who this is ...'

At this point he must have passed the phone over.

'Can you hear me, Kate? I've got to make it quick,' Ron whispered. 'I just had to talk to you, just for a minute.'

Ron didn't need to talk to me about anything in particular. I think he just wanted to hear a familiar voice. Someone who cared maybe. But that one phonecall alone cost Ron a portable television.

I continued bribing the screws for years. Or, should I say, Ron continually bribed the screws, with me carrying out Ron's orders as the middle-man.

But it all came to an abrupt end early one morning in the sleepy village of Headcorn in Kent, where I was staying with Harry, my best friend and ex-husband, in his cottage.

There was a loud bang on the front door. I ran to the bedroom window and tore the curtains open, ready to shout at whoever it was making a noise at such an ungodly hour. I took a breath and held it. I saw the two plain-clothed policemen standing in the doorway. I knew they were the Old Bill straight away. Their suits, really shabby compared to Ron's, were crumpled where they had obviously been sitting in their car waiting for me.

I called out to Harry in a hushed voice, 'It's the Old Bill. I'm not here if they want me.'

I knew it could only be trouble. I just had a gut feeling about it. When Harry opened the door they introduced themselves as being from the Thames Valley Police and asked for Mrs Kate Kray. Harry said that I was not there and that he did not know where I was. They obviously did not believe him. They said they would wait.

Harry said, 'Please your fucking selves,' then slammed the door.

The Old Bill weren't bothered. They are used to playing a waiting game. They made their way back to their unmarked police car and settled in for the long wait ahead of them.

Before I spoke to the police, I thought it was better to speak to Ron. He was bound to know what was going on.

I phoned Broadmoor straight away and got a message to Ron. He told me to give them a swerve and see him immediately.

I scoffed my breakfast and got ready for the visit.

I knew the Old Bill were still waiting for me outside the front of the house, so I decided to sneak out the back way.

But there was a problem. The back gate was jammed. There was no way out. I had no choice. There was only one thing left to do — climb over the fence. A simple thing to do if you are a ten-year-old boy, which I wasn't! I reached up and grabbed the top of the rickety wooden fence. I clutched hold of it. Something felt slimy in between my fingers. I jumped back and looked at my hands. They were covered in green moss and, to top it all, I had broken a finger nail.

I got a foot-hold in the fence, swung my leg over the top and ripped my tights on a rusty spike. There I was. Perched on the top of Harry's fence, my arse in the air and my tights torn to shreds. I was looking down the alley ready to jump down and, to my horror, standing at the end of the alley were the two police officers. Their hands were on their hips and a 'what-the-fuck-do-you-think-you're-doing?' look was written all over their faces.

'Mrs Kray, we need to talk to you,' they smirked.

What could I say? They had me 'bang to rights'.

I made an embarrassing and not very dignified jump from the top of the fence. My bag and its entire contents were strewn everywhere.

After the officers helped me retrieve my make-up bag from all over the muddy alley, they arrested me for bribery and corruption and took me to Berkshire Police Station. They questioned me for hours. While I was in custody, the police went back to Harry's and took away all the books and diaries in connection with my car-hire business.

When the officers came into the interrogation room and produced the books, I wasn't bothered. Weeks before, I had forged entries in the diary of bogus pick-ups at Heathrow Airport. I knew that I had covered myself and the bribed staff at Broadmoor, so the Old Bill wouldn't be able to prove anything. But I was very glad I had used my head and covered my arse by paying the officers from my business account.

The newspapers had a field day saying that Ronnie and I had been arrested for bribery and corruption. It was true. I had been arrested for bribery and corruption but, when the police went to interview Ron, he told them to piss off and laughed at them, saying, 'What are you going to do — put me in prison?'

He was right there was nothing the authorities could do to him. But they could do a lot to me. They went through all my bank accounts with a fine tooth comb but they drew a blank. This frustrated them as they desperately wanted to pin something on me because, by getting at me, they thought they would get at Ron.

It must be every copper's ambition to nail a Kray. Apart from adding Brownie points to their promotional prospects, I suppose it's something to brag about in the police canteen.

They investigated just about everybody and left no stone unturned. Try as they might, they didn't succeed and, boy, did they try.

After the police dropped all the charges, Ron wanted to celebrate and asked me to bring a huge sea food banquet into Broadmoor. Ron loved seafood. He often asked me to go shopping for him. I used to get him all sorts: lobster, jellied eels, tins of crab, and his favourite — tins of sardines.

I once took twelve tins of sardines in olive oil into Broadmoor. I could not imagine what the hell he wanted with all those tins of sardines, so I asked him, 'What the fuck are you doing with all those sardines?'

Ron howled with laughter. 'I'm eating them. What the fuck do you think I'm doing with them? Smothering my body in the olive oil and trying to slip through the bars?'

This was not a rare moment of fun and laughter that we shared together in Broadmoor, but probably one that Ron would repeat to many a visitor as he thought it was just so funny.

Apart from seafood, Ron also liked good clothes. It was important for him to look good because it kept his self-respect and self-esteem which he always valued.

Ron loved shoes. He thought nothing of spending £400 on crocodile shoes. I used to shop in Bond Street for them in a specialist shop called Fratelli Rossetti. Each time I went I had to buy two pairs — one black, one brown.

On one occasion I had spent nearly a grand on two pairs of crocodile shoes. They were the loafer style with two little tassels on the front. However, when Ron appeared on a visit wearing them, they were minus the tassels.

I said, 'Your shoes ... they look different. What have you done to them?'

'I've pulled those soppy tassels off,' he replied.

I shrieked 'But they cost £400 a pair.'

'It doesn't matter how much they cost, Kate, I didn't like them.'

On one of my many visits to Broadmoor, I took Ron a beautiful silk tie. I had been out shopping in the West End and had a brilliant day, so I decided I would buy Ron a little present.

I toured around the posh stores looking for something special when I eventually found a gorgeous silk tie. It was just the job and I knew Ronnie would love it.

The very next morning, I took it up to him. When you take anything into a patient in Broadmoor you are not allowed to hand the item directly to them. It has to be put in a specially designed strong box. The box is then taken on to the ward and opened in front of the patient, then searched. This is to discourage anyone from smuggling anything inside the institution.

When I arrived on my visit, I put the silk tie into the strong box. Then I made my way over to the visiting hall where Ron was waiting for me. I had told him on the telephone the night before that I had bought him a pressie. He loved presents and would get all excited.

When I reached the visiting hall, the first thing he asked me was, 'What's my pressie?'

'A lovely silk tie,' I whispered. 'It's Giorgio Armani.'

Ron's face was blank. 'Georgio Armani! Do I know him?'

'No,' I said, 'It's Georgio Armani.'

Ron still didn't know what I meant. He was so oblivious of designer labels, he asked in all innocence, 'Didn't he like the tie, then?'

I screamed with laughter. So did Ron when I explained.

A lot has been said and written about Ronnie's suits and, for a change, it was all true. Every one was hand made, each setting him back £800. His tailor went into Broadmoor to measure him up for a new one almost every month, clutching samples of cloth for Ron to choose from. His favourite tailor is a man called Barry Scott. Most of the gangsters used to have their suits made by him and still do. Barry is Saville Row trained and knew exactly how Ron liked his suits cut.

He was not only fussy about the cut of a suit but also the material it was made from. Appearance was everything to Ron. It always had been. Just because he was in prison he never let his standards slip.

Normally, he chose cashmere, navy blue, pin-striped. Mostly, he chose dark suits. But for our wedding he chose Prince of Wales check. He didn't like three-piece suits, only two, and he hated the modern trousers with pleats in the front.

I would tease him sometimes, telling him he should keep up with fashions. He would laugh and say, 'I'm stuck in my old East End ways and too old to change now. Anyway, I like those little flaps at the back of my jacket and I don't want big shoulders or long jackets. I'd feel too much like a gangster!'

He was a stubborn old sod at times. But he did have some really nice suits. One of my favourites was a silver-grey double-breasted one. He looked the business in it as he strode into the visiting room with his hands deep in his pockets. He looked like he owned the place. Even after serving 26 years in prison, he still had the ability to turn heads.

On the inside pocket of hand-made suits is the client's name and date it was made. Now, after Ron's death, I often wonder where all Ron's suits have gone. I have a couple hanging in my wardrobe, ones that he wanted cleaned which I never got around to doing. I will never have them cleaned now because they smell slightly of Ron.

Now and then I take them out of the plastic that they are wrapped in and give them a brush. If I hold them close I can still smell a slight whiff of his aftershave. In a flash, all the memories I have of my time with Ron come flooding back and I feel strangely comforted by them. Maybe the rest of his suits stayed in Broadmoor. I'm sure he would have wanted the other patients to have them. Or maybe his brother Charlie collected them all after Ron died. I just don't know.

When Ron was ill, the staff at Broadmoor allowed me to go to his room in the new block occasionally. I never went to the old block, Taunton Ward, which was like an old Victorian nut house.

There was nothing modern about it. For years, Ron had the unenviable task of slopping out. It wasn't until the beginning of 1991 that Ron was moved to the new block. The name of the ward was Abingdon. It was meant to house all the high-profile prisoners, such as Ronnie, Sutcliffe and the Stockwell Strangler.

The new Abingdon ward, opened by Princess Diana in 1991, was set apart from the old asylum, a red-brick building looking just like a Medical Centre. I asked Ron if he saw Princess Diana that day. He was disappointed and said that he had been kept well away from the Princess because he was a high-profile prisoner. The building she opened was divided into two parts. In the middle was a small visiting area, sparsely furnished with two low coffee tables and two easy chairs.

As you walked into the main entrance you went straight into the visiting area. Directly in front of you was a big window with unbreakable glass. Outside, under the window, was a huge pond filled with Koi carp. This was, I suppose, meant to be therapeutic for the patients.

You are only allowed on to the ward when the

patients are in the depths of their illness and only two patients are allowed in this visiting room at one time.

The visitors are restricted as well. You are searched more thoroughly; all sharp objects are confiscated to avoid patients inflicting injuries to themselves or others. Money was also restricted, with only enough for a cup of coffee from the staff vending machine being allowed.

The whole place is saturated with guards on full alert because they know the patients could turn violent at any time.

Ron much preferred it on Abingdon Ward. He said it was much more civilised. He even had his own toilet and wash basin in his cell.

Isn't it strange what we take for granted on the outside? When we look through a window, we sometimes don't see for looking.

When Ron first moved to Abingdon Ward, the thing he talked about for weeks was how, for the first time in over 20 years, he could look through a window without the bars. He thought it was marvellous that the glass was unbreakable, so there was no need for bars.

'I'm not like a caged animal any more,' he said.

His room was furnished quite nicely, or as well as could be expected under the circumstances. It had a peach-coloured bedspread and matching curtains and carpet. Standing in the corner was a small oak wardrobe, where, hanging neatly in rows, were Ron's suits.

On a small shelf stood his TV and video recorder. In fact, he had all the things he wanted to make his life as comfortable as possible. Perhaps I'm giving the wrong impression. All these things did not come out of the taxpayer's pockets. His room didn't come fully furnished. Ron bought everything except the bed himself.

Broadmoor patients are not normally allowed to remain in their own rooms all day. It's Broadmoor policy to get the patients out of bed and doing some kind of activity or work for most of the day. Unless they have a job, they must go into an appointed area, usually the day-room, or if the patient feels angry or upset, he can go into the quiet room to cool off..

For Ron, it was slightly different. Ron had not been off the ward for 12 years. When I visited him on one occasion the doctor asked if he could see me for a moment. He had something he wanted my help with. He thought it would be a good idea to get Ron off the ward and they needed my help to do it. They had told him that they wanted him to take a job. Ron's reply was to tell them to piss off. He said, 'I'm not weaving fucking baskets for no one.'

They also suggested that he should try to do some gardening, but he refused. They thought I might have some influence on him. When I spoke to him, I said, 'Why don't you go out into the garden and get some fresh air? You will be able to have a fag and be on your own.'

Ron thought about it and, reluctantly, he agreed. 'I'll give it one day. Just one,' he said.

He started off out on the allotment hoeing between the spring vegetables. To his surprise, he enjoyed it so much that, in the end, he was working outside for three days a week. Two days on the allotment and the other day he spent watering the plants. He continued doing this for months. He looked better for it and he loved it.

After the initial novelty wore off, Ron's idea of gardening was to sit in the sun having a fag. But at least it got him outside, although he would only do it when the weather was nice.

At that time he began a friendship with two black twin sisters called Jennifer and June Gibbons. They were known as the 'Silent Twins' because, for many years, they did not talk to anyone except each other and, when they did, no one could understand a word they said. It was as if they had a secret language and they communicated telepathically. Ron really liked them, and he used to get me to send them flowers on their birthday. He was terribly upset when one of the twins, Jennifer, died.

Ron's work experience as a gardener ended as quickly as it began. He said to me one day out of the blue, 'I'm not going to work in the gardens any more, Kate.'

I was very disappointed. He seemed so settled. 'Why not?' I asked.

He looked at me with a dead-pan expression and, in an indignant voice, he said, ' 'Cos paper boys get paid more than me. I only get £12 a week.'

I couldn't argue with that, could I?

Back on the ward, some of the other patients used to get on his nerves by asking him for cigarettes and hanging around him constantly wanting to be his friend. When he wasn't feeling too good, it drove him nuts. The staff recognised this and were good enough to allow Ron to go into his own room when, and if, he wanted to.

He didn't pay for this privilege. The staff knew when Ron needed time to be alone without being pestered. They said it was for Ron's benefit, but I really do think it was for their own. Perhaps a pacified lion is better than an angry one.

A lot has been said about Ron and his sex life. When I was first with Ron we discussed his homosexuality, but he always insisted that he was bisexual. I did not have any reason to disbelieve him. It didn't matter a damn to me. I liked him as a person. Many women loved Ron and he loved women. He didn't fancy them. He loved their company. Before he was sentenced, he nearly married a girl called Monica. She was his girlfriend for three years and he told me he really loved her.

In the past, he did used to have sex with girls but said he preferred young men.

Looking at a masculine man like Ron I found it hard to understand, but he just winked and said, 'You can't say you don't like oranges until you've tried one.'

He did like his little sayings and, more often than not, I had an answer for them.

'Well, I don't like fruit very much, and I certainly don't like fucking oranges.'

So, in a round about sort of way, it was my way of telling him that I was straight. He never asked me but I assumed he already knew. But, like most men, he found it difficult to talk about 'womanly' things. He enjoyed the softness of a woman, and the gentleness only women have.

One of the things Ron hated most was camp men. He despised them and would not tolerate any nonsense around him. He may have been homosexual, but Ron was a very masculine man.

I know he used to have sexual relationships in Broadmoor because he told me he did — often.

I knew when he was interested in someone because he would tell me to buy a Gucci man's watch. He would wink at me with a sparkle in his eye and whisper, 'A Gucci watch always works.'

He told me that many great men, such as leaders and statesmen, had been homosexuals. He quoted people like Lawrence of Arabia and Oscar Wilde.

Then, one day, right out of the blue he said to me, 'Kate, you have got one chance to ask me any question you like about my sexuality and I will give you a straight answer.'

Knowing he was serious that I would only get one shot to ask him really personal questions, I had to be careful not to go in too strong. So, initially, I asked skirting questions like what sort of men he liked. He said he preferred men in their early 20s, slim and good looking. Then I asked him the big question, one that had been bothering me and, I'm sure, everyone else.

I wasn't sure how to put it. I did not want to ask the question in a vulgar or crude way, but how do you ask someone in a polite way if they are the dominant partner in a relationship or if they are they are the passive one? There was only one thing for it, so I just blurted it out.

'Are you the giver or the taker?'

For a moment, Ron said nothing. Then a broad smile spread across his face.

'The giver, Kate, only the giver,' he whispered.

Up until that moment, I always found it difficult to imagine Ron with another man but, when he said he was the 'giver', a million pictures flashed through my mind. I threw my hands up and my facial expression said it all. There are just some things that don't require an answer.

I suppose the reason why he had said I could ask him anything I wanted on that occasion was because he had a little piece of crumpled paper in his pocket. He rummaged about in his pocket and handed it to me. Carefully, I unfolded it. It was the result of an AIDS test. 'Negative'. I looked at him and he smiled.

'I knew you would never ask me to have a test, so I thought I would surprise you.'

I could see that he was in a good mood and was open to more questions. I was on a roll, so I decided to make the most of it. I thought I would chance my arm and ask him if he had ever snogged any of the blokes he went with. He looked at me and scowled. I couldn't imagine Ronnie kissing another man but I felt compelled to ask. He looked at me in complete disgust and snapped, 'Leave it out, Kate. I have never kissed a man.'

I suppose the Gucci watches Ron bought to seduce his conquests inevitably worked because the watches always disappeared. I never got any of them back. I imagine half of the patients in Broadmoor walking about wearing Gucci watches, or at least the young men among them.

On one of our visits he told me he had his eye on this black boy called Mohammed. He was on the same ward as Ron. Mohammed was a tall, good-looking lad in his early 20s.

Ron was smitten with him. Every day he would go to the shower block to watch Mohammed take a shower. This went on for months and months.

When I used to go on a visit, after we got business out of the way we talked about everyday things. The subject eventually got round to Mohammed in the shower.

Ron never used to take a shower at the same time as him, but he would just happen to be in the shower block. He took great delight in watching the water run down Mohammed's black skin. His eyes shone when he talked about him.

'All those little droplets of water running down his black body looks so beautiful,' Ron said.

Then, one day, he whispered to me, 'Get me a Gucci, Kate.'

I knew then that Ron had made progress with

Mohammed. Black, brown or even yellow, Ron didn't care about the colour of anyone's skin. He wasn't prejudiced and would not tolerate anyone around him who was.

Some of the people Ron met, he liked. Some he despised. One man Ron despised was Ron Saxon. My Ron had three black friends in the hospital. Mohammed was one of them, the other two being Cleveland Jones and Paul Wilson.

They were not only Ron's friends but also Saxon's. Saxon would use them to fetch and carry for him, especially after he suffered a heart-attack. They really liked him and Ron obviously thought that Saxon appreciated what they did for him.

But one day, when Ron commented to Saxon about how good they'd been to him, Saxon merely said, 'They're black bastards. They're OK, but only good enough to be used.'

Ron was horrified. Racial prejudice was one of the things he hated most in the world.

He told me that if Saxon had been a younger man, he would have hurt him. After that, Ron — my Ron — would have nothing to do with him. Saxon had a second heart-attack and died, and Ron refused to go to the funeral at Broadmoor. The only people who went were the three black boys.

'It just goes to show,' said Ron. 'It just proves to me how ignorant people can be, however old they are. They get old and they are still ignorant. I hate fascists. If Ron Saxon can see from beyond the grave — and I think he can — he would have seen those three coloured boys coming back to the ward after paying their respects to him at his funeral. And he would have seen tears in their eyes.'

It upset Ron a lot and it prompted him to write this poem:

We are all born the same
From God we all came
Coloured, White or Jew
We are all God's children, not just a few
We should all be brothers
And think of others
Then, to God, we will all be true.

Coming from a half-caste family myself, I also hate racial discrimination. Looking back on it now, I think that Ron and I had a lot in common. That is probably why we got on so well. Not only were our views on lots of subjects the same, but I made him laugh when everyone else around him was always so serious.

When I first met Ron, he never used to smile much. He always took things so seriously. I remember the first time I actually saw him cry — with laughter.

We were talking about whether or not men or women could bear the most pain. Ron insisted that men were the stronger sex. I disagreed. I looked down at his strong fist. Right across the top was a deep red scar. I asked him how he got it. He looked at me out of the corner of his eye and smirked. 'To prove a point,' he whispered.

He explained that one night he put a red-hot poker on a man's face, prompting someone to remark that Ron could give pain but not take it. He was furious when he heard that. Later that night at the pub, Ron was determined to make a point. He put his hand on the bar, pulled out a big knife and stabbed the razor-sharp blade deep into the back of his hand. Without flinching, he proceeded to tear it open, severing the veins. Blood splattered everywhere.

'Yuk! That's disgusting,' I said. 'But women can

stand more pain than that, especially this woman. Look, I'll show ya.'

I held my hand out in front of him.

Ron looked puzzled. He had been inside for so long he knew nothing about false finger nails. I took hold of the nails one by one and proceeded to rip them out of my finger tips. Ron winced and covered his eyes as each nail fell into the ashtray.

'Stop it, stop it,' he cringed.

I laughed. 'Do you give in? Can women stand more pain than men?'

'They are not real finger nails. What the fuck are they?' Ron asked.

I handed him an inch-long painted nail.

'Well, I never,' he sighed. 'What's happening in the world? False finger nails, eh? You little fucker, Kate,' he laughed.

That's one thing Ron never lacked — humour. We laughed together a lot.

When the BSE beef scare was in all the newspapers, he could not wait for me to go on a visit. As I walked towards him in the visiting hall, he said, 'Kate, Kate, I am never going to eat beef again. You know why? Because it drives you mad!'

I looked at him. I could not believe what he had just said.

'But, Ron, you're already mad ... you're in Broadmoor.'

He scowled for a minute. I thought he was going to go into one. Then his eyes softened and a broad smile lit up his face,

'Oh yeah,' he laughed.

But through all the laughter, never for one moment did I doubt the power and the influence that Ron wielded in Broadmoor.

On the rare occasion that Ron and I argued, it

was normally at a time when he was not feeling well. I could always tell by his eyes. They say that your eyes are the windows to your soul, and I believe it to be true. Ron's eyes told me a lot, especially when he wasn't well.

Ron didn't need telling, as he always recognised his own illness before any one else and would usually cancel all his visits — except mine. He did this not only because he did not like people seeing him when he was ill, but because he became paranoid and didn't trust anybody. He hated that side of his illness.

At these times he became quite demanding, usually asking me to do lots of running around.

'Go and see Reggie in Leicester and tell him ...' he would demand. 'Go and pick up a package at Heathrow ...' These were not things you could do in an hour, they would usually take all day.

He once joked with me, 'Before we married, I would ask you to do things. Now we are married, I'll tell you.'

Although he said it as a joke, I think, in a way, he meant it.

On one particular occasion when he wasn't well, he had asked me to do loads of things. He gave me lists and lists of things to do. People to see. Places to go.

At the best of times I am quite a forgetful person. That's one of the reasons I always wrote things down, and why I had so many bloody lists. You can bet your life I might do fourteen things on the list but the fifteenth one would be the most important and ... guess what? That was the one I should have done first.

One particular day, I could see Ron wasn't very well. Gingerly, I started going through his list with him.

'Yes, I delivered that package.'

'Yes, I picked up your suit from the cleaners.'

'Yes, I arranged all your visits.'

Things were going well, until we got to the last thing on the list. I didn't think it was that important. It was only something trivial, but I hadn't done it. His eyes changed. They went black with anger. In an instant, he snapped.

'Why didn't you do that? It was the most important thing on the list ...'

I had never seen him so angry. He said some awful things to me. I got very upset and started to cry. We ended up having a right old barny. Being a woman, I did what all women do and threatened to leave.

He told me to sit down and wipe my eyes. Just for one minute I thought he was going to apologise. I was wrong. He reached over and whispered in my ear. I was shocked. He didn't say much, but what he did say was said with such venom. He said that if I tried to leave him, he would have me taken care of. I knew exactly what he meant by that.

Still not taking him seriously, I said that none of his friends would ever hurt me as they all liked me. He went quiet and sniggered. He didn't raise his voice; he didn't have to.

'You silly girl, don't you think I know that? I would get one of the nutters in here who was on home leave to take care of it. They would do anything for me. Remember, Kate, they have got nothing to lose.'

I was shocked. First, I never thought Ron would ever threaten me. Second, I knew he was right about the people in Broadmoor. They would do anything for him. I had had a bad experience in the past with an obsessed nutter stalking me. His name was Frank

Butler. A name I'll never forget.

Ron had given Butler's wife my name, address and phone number for some reason, and Butler was soon to be released from Broadmoor after serving 18 years.

It was Christmas 1990. My phone kept ringing morning, noon and night. Every time I picked it up, it was the same person — Butler.

He sounded odd — it wasn't his Geordie accent, but he would say strange things.

At first he just paid me veiled compliments, like how he liked me and how lucky Ron was to have me as his wife. Then he started to get a little more serious, drooling, and wondering why didn't I let him take care of me sexually because Ron was in prison and he was out.

Then he blatantly asked if he could have sex with me. I got really angry. How dare he take such a liberty? I snapped at him, 'Don't you dare talk to me like that otherwise I will tell Ron.'

From that moment his mood changed. Things turned ugly. The phonecalls were no longer polite — they were filth.

He said that he would cut the tendons in the back of my legs if I didn't have sex with him. The phonecalls carried on for three days. Day and night the phone never stopped ringing. It was starting to drive me crazy. Every time I picked the phone up, it was him. In one day alone he had rung 32 times. I was at the end of my tether.

The phone rang again. I snatched it off the hook and screamed, 'Leave me alone.'

This time it was Reggie on the phone. 'What is the matter with you, Kate?' he asked.

I told him all about the filthy phonecalls and asked him to phone the filthy pervert to tell him to leave me alone.

Reg pointed out, 'It would do no good me phoning him, because he knows you are married to Ron and that didn't stop him making the calls in the first place. Don't take any chances. He is obviously a nutter. Phone Broadmoor and tell them what is going on and then phone the police immediately.'

For Reggie to tell me to phone the police, I realised it must be extremely serious. I rang Broadmoor and told them what was happening. They told me to go straight to the police. The urgency in their voice convinced me to act fast, so I went straight to the police station in Maidstone. I felt embarrassed telling them that I was Ronnie Kray's wife and that a nutter was after me. They were very sympathetic and took some notes. I thought a visit from the Old Bill would be enough to stop him, but I soon found out just how wrong I was.

By the time I got home, I couldn't believe it. There were Old Bill everywhere. I pulled my car up outside my house and a burly policewoman ushered me inside.

She told me that they had spoken to Broadmoor and they said that Frank Butler was one of the most dangerous men they had ever held there.

The police insisted that I go to a safe house. I thought they were going over the top a bit, but I suppose they knew best. Pressure pads were installed under the carpets in my home just in case he managed to get in.

DI Pat Geary, the officer in charge of the case, stayed in my house and pretended that she was me. Butler was obviously mentally ill. But he still kept ringing. I was glad that he was talking to the policewoman and not to me. He even threatened to kill her, still thinking that it was me. The police in Newcastle-upon-Tyne, his home town, were notified, but Butler was nowhere to be found.

Everyone was concerned. It was a waiting game. They all knew it was only a matter of time before he surfaced. They didn't have to wait long. It was the following day when the police picked him up in Maidstone town centre. He had come all the way from Newcastle-upon-Tyne to kill me.

To look at him, you would think that butter wouldn't melt in his mouth. He didn't have horns sticking out of the top of his head or 'rapist' tattooed on his forehead. That was the trouble — he just looked normal, or as normal as can be for a 65-year-old wearing a cheap wig. Pat Geary made me laugh when she said he looked more like an old granddad rather than an evil rapist. She said that when they were interviewing him, he was really placid and softly spoken. But when they went to take his wig off to photograph him, he went mad, shouting and screaming at the officers. She said he was like a wild man.

I did laugh when she said that but, in reality, it was not funny. Neither was his criminal record. It turned out that his record was as long as your arm, starting way back in 1945. He had a history of indecently assaulting women and young girls.

Indeed, he was sentenced to 18 years in Broadmoor for cutting the tendons in the back of a young girl's legs — exactly what he had threatened to do to me. After his arrest, I went up to visit Ron and he said, 'Frank Butler is a dangerous man, so when it goes to court you must attend to give evidence.'

He explained that if I refused and he went on to hurt somebody elses — someone not as strong as me — I would never forgive myself. Of course, he was right.

When the day came to go to court, I went. The charge was threatening to murder. I agreed that he should be let off with a caution because, while on bail, he had stabbed somebody and the police wanted the higher charge of attempted murder. I hope he is still away somewhere and remains there indefinitely. But I don't think he ever went back to Broadmoor because, if Ron could have got to him, he would have killed him.

*   *   *

Long before Ron and I were married, I decided that I would try to make Ron's life as happy and comfortable as I possibly could in Broadmoor, even if that meant putting my own liberty at risk. It was not difficult to get Ronnie the five-star treatment, and one of the treats I organised was a 'seafood banquet whenever Reggie came to visit him.

Ron always liked to put something special on for Reggie. It wasn't well known that Reggie was allowed internal visits every three months. They enjoyed these times just sitting, eating and chatting about all the business and old times, whilst sipping Kaliber non-alcoholic lager.

If there was any of the food left over, the twins would insist that it went to the other patients, just to give them a little bit extra.

I never knew when Reggie was going to visit Ron, it was all kept very hush hush because of the security aspect. Reggie was always handcuffed inside the prison van. It didn't matter if, at the time, he was being held in Leicester Prison or Parkhurst on the Isle of Wight.

The officers would spirit him out under cover and then spirit him back again before anyone could find out. You just never knew when he was going to visit Ron until the day before, or even sometimes the same day. I didn't always have time to take the food up, so I would phone the catering manager at Broadmoor to organise something and pay for it by cheque on the next visit.

They used to leave the bill at the gate house and I'd settle up when I got there. Ron loved those times he had with Reggie alone. The following day, he would eagerly tell me all about their visit.

In all my years with Ron, I never saw the twins together. I would have loved to have seen them sitting in the visiting hall together eating lobster, sipping beer and arguing.

Internal visits with Reggie were one of the few pleasures that Ronnie had left, and God knows he didn't have many. I asked him once, if he was allowed out for one day, what would he most like to do?

I expected him to want to go to the pub and get sozzled or do some wild and wacky thing. But he didn't. He sighed.

'If I had one day of freedom — just one — I would love to walk in a park in springtime, when the bluebells and daffodils are in full bloom, and to stroke a dog.'

It nearly broke my heart. Something so simple. One that we on the outside take for granted.

In one of Ronnie's more lethargic moods, he once told me that he thought it would have been kinder to hang him. He felt being locked away for so many years was like a slow torture. What a strange twist of fate. Long ago, when Ron was a boy, he asked his Aunt Rose why his eyebrows met in the middle. She replied, 'That means you are born to hang, Ronnie, love.'

5

Great Escape

Ron never managed to escape from Broadmoor, except through death, but it was often on his mind.

He made his first daring escape from prison just after Christmas in 1957, and what a spectacular one it was, too. The great escape artist, Houdini, could have learnt a lesson or two from him.

In November 1956, Ronnie received a three-year prison sentence for grievous bodily harm. The twins had become involved in a dispute between the owner of a West End drinking club called The Stragglers and a rival Irish gang. The Irishmen wanted to take over the bar. The club owner however, had other ideas and turned to Reg and Ron for protection. He wanted the Krays to stamp out the fighting that plagued his bar, and Ron was more than happy to oblige — for the right fee of course.

Ronnie was in his element and wasted no time going to the club to confront the Irishmen. That evening was one to remember. All hell broke loose between the tough Irishmen and Ronnie's firm. It resembled something out of the Wild West, a bar-room brawl, chairs being thrown at mirrors, shots being fired into the ceiling, kicking and gouging in the blood and the beer.

There were lots of casualties. Needless to say, Ron walked away totally unscathed, just like John Wayne always did. The cowboy he fought and beat almost to death was called Terence Martin, for which Ron received his prison sentence of three years.

The separation from Reggie was a great emotional blow to Ronnie. On the other hand, it gave Reggie a free reign to manage the twins' business interests in his own way without Ronnie's demands for violent retribution at the faintest hint of an insult or competition. Reggie was good and business boomed.

One of his first moves was to open a legitimate club called the Double R on the Bow Road that soon became the East End's premier night-spot. At the same time, he moved into minding and protecting the illegal gambling parties held at smart addresses in Mayfair and Belgravia.

But Ronnie was never very far from Reggie's mind. Hence the name of the club, The Double R, short for Reg and Ron.

Ronnie accepted his sentence at Wandsworth Prison and bided his time. He was always treated with respect by his fellow inmates, many of whom he already knew. He was reasonably settled but, unexpectedly, he was transferred to Camp Hill Prison on the Isle of Wight. That was a bolt out of the blue for Ronnie. He hated Camp Hill and felt isolated, being so far away from his family in the East End.

Ronnie's illness — then in its early stages — took a turn for the worse just after Christmas 1957 when he heard that his favourite Aunt Rose had died. Ronnie went crazy. He felt helpless, unable to comfort his mum or, more importantly, to be comforted himself.

He released his frustrations in the only way he knew how — through violence. Often, men smash things up when they are angry. Ron was no different. He demolished the wing and knocked out everybody who stood in his way. The screws were quick to act. It took eight of them to hold him down and still they struggled to put him into a canvas strait-jacket. He kicked and cursed the lot of them.

The following morning, Ronnie was certified insane.

He was transferred to Long Hill, a psychiatric hospital in Epsom, Surrey. With the proper medical treatment, Ronnie's condition rapidly improved.

Every Sunday, visitors came to see their friends or relatives. Reggie, naturally, was a regular visitor. While he could see that Ronnie was on the road to recovery, he knew that if the hospital continued to regard Ronnie as insane, they could postpone his release date indefinitely. There was nothing for it; Ronnie had to escape.

The security was strict, but there had to be a way. The twins noticed that, for some reason, little attention was paid to Sunday afternoon visitors. They developed a plan which was ingenious, but so simple.

On the day of the escape, Reggie came to visit Ron at the hospital wearing an overcoat. Even though it was a warm afternoon nobody seemed to notice. Reggie sat down at the small Formica table, slipped off his overcoat and whispered to Ron. Ronnie smirked and gave a knowing nod and the plan swung into action.

The patients were not allowed to approach the tea counter, only the visitors were. Under the noses of the guards, Ronnie got up and ordered two hot steaming cups of tea.

Reggie slowly moved over on to Ronnie's seat, all the time aiming to look inconspicuous. He began by unbuttoning the collar of his blue shirt and rolling up his sleeves trying to look as casual as possible. Ronnie returned and put the teas on the table and sat down in Reggie's seat. As he did, he slipped his arms into Reggie's overcoat. Nobody noticed again. The switch was made. Cool as a cucumber the twins sipped their tea and finished their visit.

'Time's up, finish your visit, please,' the screw called.

Ronnie stood up and walked through the door to freedom.

By the time they clocked that the remaining twin was Reggie, Ronnie was safely on his way to a caravan in Suffolk owned by Geoff Allen.

Geoff was an old friend of the twins and was said to be the brains behind the Great Train Robbery as reported in the newspapers. Ronnie looked up to him as a father figure and was devastated by his death on Christmas Day 1994. There was talk at the time of Reg and Ron attending his funeral. However, Ronnie was denied permission to attend because of the security aspect. He sent me instead.

It was early January. Snow was thick on the ground. The service was scheduled for early morning. I pulled on some thick black tights and a black dress. Ronnie wanted me to wear the full-length, white fox-fur coat that he had just bought me and I was glad he insisted because it was freezing cold at the time. I was running late, mainly because my car would not start and the bad weather and all the snow on the road made my journey slower. Frantically, I looked at my watch. Shit! I was very late. By the time I had reached the small graveyard in the middle of the Suffolk countryside, everybody was in the church.

I knew there were a number of important and famous people going including Bill Wyman of the Rolling Stones. Geoff sold his house to him and they became friends. Geoff was so popular there were hundreds of mourners inside the church. Outside the church however, standing like frozen snowmen, were dozens of photographers, TV crews and minders in their obligatory black overcoats.

As I ran down the winding footpath to the church entrance, I hummed a song under my breath.

'I'm late, I'm late, for a very important date ...'

As I approached the minders, I waved my hands and called, 'No time to say hello, good-bye, I'm late, I'm late, I'm late.'

They looked at each other, then raised their eyes to heaven and let me through.

I was in such a panic because I was late, I entered via the wrong door. To my horror, I went in the side entrance that led directly in front of the altar — and the coffin. The door slammed behind me. For a moment I heard the voice of Frank Sinatra singing 'I Did It My Way'. I froze and looked at the solemn congregation. The look on their faces said it all. There I was, standing beside the vicar. Him in his long white robes and me in my long, white fur coat.

Geoff Allen would have forgiven me, I'm sure. We shared a mutual love and respect for each other which was so special.

Geoff was one of the few people whom Ronnie truly trusted when he was paranoid. That's probably why he stayed at Geoff's caravan in Suffolk after his escape in 1957. It was thought that the peace and quiet would be all Ron needed to help him on the road to recovery. They were right. Ron loved the isolation of the countryside, prompting him later to buy a huge white-washed mansion in Suffolk. Ron whiled away his new-found freedom walking in the countryside like a true country gent.

He had to stay long enough for his certification of insanity to expire, and then he went back to the police and gave himself up to complete his sentence in Wandsworth Prison. He was finally released in 1958.

It wasn't often that Ron got one over on the authorities, but he felt his escape was a coup. This prompted him to help any inmate in any way he could if they harboured thoughts of escape.

This was the case when another patient called Dennis Grant wanted to escape from Broadmoor. It was all arranged that he would disappear from an outside working party. An outside works party is where inmates are taken out of the confines of Broadmoor to work. They worked in the community, thinking it would integrate them back into society.

Ron handed me a crumpled piece of paper.

'Don't read it now. Wait 'til you get outside,' he whispered.

I took the note and put it in my handbag. I didn't ask any questions. By the way he spoke and the secretive way he passed me the note, I knew the message was hot.

As I got up to leave, Ron gently whispered in my ear, 'Send a grand to the address Kate — used notes.'

I did not like sending cash through the post. I offered to take it.

'Just do as I tell you,' Ron snapped.

Normally, if the money I had to pass on to someone was a large amount, I would meet them at a tube station or some out-of-the-way place and hand it to them directly. I did this for two reasons. One, the cash could go astray legitimately in the post; and two, some of the villains who were receiving the money were, shall we say, a little less than honest!

On this occasion, Ron was adamant that I was not to do any of that. I had to put £1,000 in a plain brown envelope without a note and send it off to the address that was scribbled on the piece of paper. I addressed the envelope to a girl called Yvonne. No last name, just an address.

In the past I have sent lots of plain brown packages to people I had never heard of. This time I had a bad feeling. I don't know what it was. Call it a gut reaction. Maybe it was the fact that for the first time Ronnie didn't tell me what was going on, which was unusual for him. He never kept me in the dark about anything. He would say nothing, only that he would tell me everything in a couple of days. He was very secretive. I sensed that he was getting a buzz from whatever it was.

I did what I was told. I withdrew the money from the hole in the wall at the Woolwich Building Society where I held Ron's account. I put the used notes in a buff-coloured envelope. I slid bits of card down the side so that it didn't feel like money and sent it off.

I have to admit that I was curious to know what the money was for. I didn't have to wait long. A few days later, there it was on the early evening news.

It made the headline news that an inmate had escaped from Broadmoor while out on a works party. I knew then exactly what the money was for.

Next time I saw Ron, he gave me a knowing smile. I asked him if that was what the bundle of cash was for.

'I'll leave that as a rhetorical question, Kate,' he smirked.

*　　　　*　　　　*

After I married Ronnie Kray, the only people I seemed to have any dealings with were gangsters. All my friends were gangsters — still are, most of them. Therefore, it was easy to get sucked into the criminal underworld. Crime became a way of life for me. Before I knew it, I became involved in all sorts of skulduggery. I started to become entangled in situations which I would have otherwise avoided like the plague. At times, I even found myself in strange disguises doing odd things that were completely out of character for me.

That's exactly what happened early in the summer of 1994.

The phone rang one morning. It must have been early because it was still dark outside. It was a friend of Ron's called Big Buff — not his real name, of course. He earned his nickname because he is the size of a buffalo and twice as wild.

'Don't say anything, Kate. Remember, walls have ears,' he snarled.

I knew when I heard Big Buff's voice that I would be going on a trip. A call from Big Buff usually meant a trip, one that might lead me into trouble.

We arranged to meet on a roundabout off the M25 at junction 10. I drove to Surrey where the boys were waiting.

I recognised Larry sitting in the car, otherwise known as 'Loose Lips Larry' because he didn't think before he spoke.

Big Buff stood by the motor to keep watch. I pulled my car up beside them and wound the window down.

Buff winked. 'Follow us, Kate.'

I followed their BMW for about half-a-mile to a wooded picnic area. We circled the car park a couple of times before parking away from the tourists and day-trippers. I locked my small white hatchback and climbed into the back seat of their BMW. Buff looked around nervously. Speaking out of the corner of his mouth, as most gangsters do, he hissed, 'We got a job for ya, Kate — a big one.'

He explained that a Dutchman called Hans had been sentenced to 15 years' imprisonment for drug smuggling. Hans wanted out. Buff and Larry were going to spring him. They had been working on the escape for months. It had all been arranged. The Dutchman had been writing to a fake address and to a pretend girlfriend. The correspondence was kept up for three months. Nobody suspected anything. It's one thing writing to a moody girlfriend, but the time had now arrived for the moody girlfriend to materialise — and, of course, they wanted me to be the moody girlfriend!

Buff continued, 'I want you to have a snapshot taken in a disguise — it will be worth your while.'

I furrowed my eyebrows. I was confused, 'What sort of disguise?'

Buff let out a raucous laugh. 'Any kind you like — I'll leave it to your imagination.'

I told them I would have to clear it with Ron first.

Larry interrupted. 'Sorted. Ron's cleared it.'

Earlier that day, they had been to visit Ron and asked his permission to involve me. He only had two questions that he wanted answered. One: what was the likelihood of me being nicked? And two: how much he was going to get out of it? He didn't want to know the details of the job. He never did. But for Ron to allow anyone to get me involved, it must have cost them dear.

The boys went on explaining about Hans. They wanted me to go into the prison disguised as the moody girlfriend to pass on all the information about the breakout.

'What sort of information?' I asked quietly.

Buff laughed, 'Like how fucking much it will cost the goon.'

The very next evening, I went to Asda in Bexleyheath where I knew they had a passport photo booth. I was wearing a curly wig and glasses and looked more like a clown than an inconspicuous prison visitor. It was a Friday evening and the place was packed. What a time to choose. I caught a glimpse of myself in the small mirror on the side of the booth. I didn't recognise myself. Shoppers with laden trolleys were milling around, but to me it seemed as though they were all waiting for my photos to come out of the machine. I was getting paranoid. Four minutes later, the photographs slid out. I snatched them from the rollers and stuffed them in my bag before they were even dry.

I had to send the photograph to a wine bar in Surrey from where it was duly passed on to the Dutchman in prison. I bet he was really disappointed when he received the photograph. He was probably expecting a young dolly bird. Instead he got Ronald McDonald. I imagined his face opening the letter and looking at the picture. Instead of saying 'What a corker' in Dutch, he probably said, 'I'll have a cheeseburger, fries and a strawberry milkshake to take out!'

Letters were exchanged between the Dutchman and the moody girlfriend for a couple of months. I didn't read them so I hadn't a clue what was written in any of them. Then, out of the blue on a Tuesday morning, I got the call I had been waiting for.

A gruff voice said, 'We're on. The visit is arranged for Thursday.'

'Oh shit!' I replied. That didn't give me much time. Two days later, I was on my way to Surrey to meet the boys. I pulled my car up beside them and noticed that they tried not to snigger. We drove to a secluded area where a stolen car was waiting. It made sense not to use our own car just in case there were any security cameras on the boundaries of the prison which clocked the number plate.

Outside the nick, they gave me my instructions.

I was to tell him that, yes, they could get him out, and that it would cost him £100,000 worth of soap bars (cannabis) to be delivered to Dover where our boys would be waiting.

I began to feel nervous. There I was, all ready to meet a powerful drugs baron, someone I had never met before, someone I knew nothing about and I had to deliver such an important message. Everything hung on me delivering the message properly. There was a great deal at stake. I knew I had to get it right. But before that, I had to run the gauntlet of the prison security. I did not know what to expect. Maybe they would recognise me. After all, my face had been splashed all over the newspapers having just married Ron. Or maybe they had been tipped off. I was becoming increasingly paranoid. I felt sick to my stomach and, for the first time, I wondered what sort of a world I had been sucked into.

I made the final adjustments to my curly wig, took a deep breath and walked into the reception area. I handed my visitor's order to the burly screw at the desk. He didn't look up.

I felt frozen to the spot. I could hear the whirring of the security camera just above me. I had to fight the urge not to look up knowing that then they would have a clear image of my face. Visions of *Crimewatch* flashed through my mind. Nervously, I fiddled with my wig hoping it was still on straight.

'Through that gate,' the officer shouted and pointed to the heavy iron gates directly in front of me. Another screw let me in and slammed the gate shut behind me. My heart was in my mouth. I still had half-an-hour to wait.

I went through the security checks OK and was eventually led to table number 8. It was a busy day and the visiting hall was packed. There were screaming kids and snogging couples all around. For me, the wait for Hans took for ever.

Every time the prisoner door opened, I looked up

wondering if it was him. I hadn't a clue what he looked like and did not know what to expect. At least he knew who he was meeting. It was another half-an-hour before my man came in. I realised it was him when he looked at me, bit his lip and smirked. I knew then, definitely, that the curly wig was a big mistake.

He was older than I had expected; in his 50s, small, with sandy-coloured hair. He was wearing a blue round-necked, prison-issue jumper. He smiled. I stood up and with an outstretched hand said, 'You must be Hans?'

He looked at me with a blank stare. He didn't understand a word I said. The boys told me it was going to be a simple job just to pass on the message. Simple, my arse! That couldn't be further from the truth because he didn't speak any English. Well, hardly any, and he seemed to understand even less. He sat down at the small stained table.

I was supposed to be his girlfriend and in love with him but there was no way I was going to kiss him. All I wanted to do was give him the message and go, but I knew I had to make it look good.

I began by asking him if he wanted a cup of tea or coffee, maybe a cold drink. A packet of crisps, a slice of cake? He looked at me blankly. I wasn't getting through. I was getting irritable ... 'What the fuck do you want?' I got him a packet of Rolos and a plastic cup of lemonade. There he was, Mr Big — eating Rolos and sipping lemonade with a Ronald McDonald lookalike. It was crazy.

But there was more to come. I had to give him the message. But how? I wished I had known he didn't speak English; I could have been more prepared. What a day. What was I doing here? My wig wouldn't stay on straight and all he kept saying was, 'Eh ... eh ... no understand.'

I tried writing it down. After all, he must have understood written English from the letters. But then I got paranoid. So I tore the note into little bits and ate it! He must have thought I was a raving loony but I made sure he read the note before I destroyed it.

I told him to mull it over and that we would be in touch. I stood up and went to shake his hand. He had other ideas and went to kiss me. I pulled away — a snog was out the question. The guards looked over. I had to do something so I pretended we had had a row and walked off in a huff.

I couldn't wait to get out of the nick and, more importantly, out of my disguise. When I got outside, the boys were circling the car park on tenterhooks, like piranha fish at feeding time. They hated being near a prison because, I suppose, they had spent so much time inside themselves.

When I got into the car, they wanted to know every single word that had been said. I began by repeating 'no understand' and how it was all a bit of a anti-climax. I finished off by saying that he was mulling it over and he would be in touch.

We returned to our own cars and went our separate ways. I heard nothing for over a month. Then I got a call.

'We're on again,' Buff said. 'Meet us tomorrow, same place. Don't say a word. Remember, phones have ears.'

The following day, I met them at the same place. To my amazement, the plan had moved on somewhat. Buff had made a couple of trips to Amsterdam.

Things were more organised. They even told me they would pay me an extra 10% of whatever they got, once it had been converted into money, so long as I took care of the Dutchman. Easier said than done.

The plan had come on in leaps and bounds. I had to tell him to be at a fence number on a certain day and time. Prison fences are numbered. This enables the riot officers to know precisely which part of the prison is being infiltrated or escaped from during an alert.

I pulled on the ghastly wig again, hopefully for the last time. At least I knew what he looked like now, but I felt uneasy. Something wasn't right. Ron always told me that if I felt something was wrong, don't do it. Again, I went through the security checks. Then the waiting began. I waited an hour but he didn't show up. I didn't want to ask the screw if there was a problem because I didn't want to draw attention to myself. So I got up and left.

The boys were stomping mad.

'It's a fucking liberty,' they screamed.

I was hoping and praying that that would be the last I would hear of the Dutchman. I was wrong.

A couple of days later, I had the phonecall to say it was on again.

I went back to the prison feeling even more paranoid than ever. I was sure the Dutchman was a plant. If I was caught aiding and abetting an escape from prison, especially someone of his calibre, then I would be looking at ten years. Suddenly, the enormity of it dawned on me and I was not at all happy. This time, I was shown into the visiting hall and taken to table number 10. I ran my fingers round the edge of the table checking that it wasn't bugged.

Hans came in. He looked normal enough but you can never tell. Maybe his disguise was better than mine and he was, after all, an undercover cop.

I wasn't interested in pleasantries. I didn't want any tea. I wanted to cut the crap and get on with business. I told him straight. Be at fence number 7 on 17 August at 3.00pm.

In prison, for the right price, you can buy any job you like. The Dutchman was loaded and had already bought a job that enabled him to be outside at that particular time of day. Without being aggressive towards him, I had to stress the importance of the soap bars being delivered on time. I was in no mood for games and, despite the language barrier, he got the message.

When I got outside, the boys were nowhere to be seen. We had been to the nick so often that they would not even drive into the car park. I walked to the end of the road. Suddenly, they appeared and screeched to a halt in front of me. I clambered into the back of the car, pulling my wig off as we sped away.

By this time, I'd had enough. I told them that I had given him the message but that was it. I wanted no more to do with it. That was the last I heard of the Dutchman and I took great delight in burning that curly wig. I never found out if Hans escaped or not, but I do know that a few months later someone was sprung from nick. Maybe it was Hans. I don't know and I don't really care.

One escape attempt I did care about was the one that Ron planned for himself. Ron had been inside for 26 years and could not see any glimmer of hope for his release. Even though Ronnie's stay in Broadmoor was luxurious compared to the régime he would have faced in an ordinary jail, he constantly harboured thoughts of escape. Reg, on the other hand, was serving his time in a normal prison and always had some hope of parole.

Ronnie's plan to escape was an elaborate one. It took months and months of planning in this country and America. There was never any chance of Ronnie ever escaping from Broadmoor hospital and he knew it. The security there was far too tight. It had to be when he wasn't in Broadmoor.

The only time that Ronnie left Broadmoor was when he was physically ill. This didn't happen very often as Ron was quite fit. He had had an ear operation but the operation was conducted under a local anaesthetic so he was whisked straight back to Broadmoor the same day. That proved useless. However, as luck would have it, Ron had a hernia. That definitely meant he would be taken to a hospital on the outside and have to stay in for a few days. Perfect, just the break we wanted.

Ron went on a waiting list at Heatherwood Hospital in Ascot. Thank goodness for the NHS waiting lists. It was brilliant because it gave him time to make all the necessary arrangements. The planning involved many people but only Ron's closest friends knew the details. Each stage was plotted with extreme care — the plan had to be watertight, and there couldn't be any slip-ups. This was the only time that anyone would have a chance of getting Ron out. It was all arranged. In October 1992, while Ron was in hospital having his hernia operation, two Mafia men would fly into London and get him out. This wasn't a problem. The Yanks owed Ron a favour.

He had helped them out a year before by looking

after one of their hit-men who was on the run. Ron paid for him to have a new identity and a pub in London. He is still there now.

Ron called in the favour, and the Americans had to repay the debt. The two Mafia men were professionals. They were going to pose as hospital porters. Once inside the hospital, they were going to garrotte the two screws who were guarding Ron.

Ron said they would use that method as opposed to shooting them because of the noise. Even if they used a silencer, someone still might hear. I asked Ron to describe garrotting. He laughed.

'It's like cutting butter with a hot knife,' he said.

He described the thin cheese wire in great detail.

'It's wrapped around the neck,' he explained. 'It's quick but not painless!'

Ron tried to keep me out of the frame as much as he could by asking me to get involved only when it was absolutely necessary.

I made a few calls to America just to confirm a few details — names and rendezvous. Ron referred to America as 'across the pond'. He never said 'America' just in case someone overheard. He trusted no one, but I always knew what he meant.

The contact across the pond was a man called Joey. For my own safety, I will not reveal any more about Joey. He is a very powerful and dangerous man, although he trusts me completely. The police have quizzed me before about Ron and Joey's involvement and I have said nothing. For this, I was rewarded with a present. Ron gave me a diamond Cartier ring and took great delight in slipping the dazzling ring on my little finger. I never take it off.

The time for Ron's operation was approaching. All the fake documents and passports had been arranged. There was even talk of a plastic surgeon carrying out some work on Ron's face, but I don't think it would have got that far. The plan was that they'd put Ron in a wheelchair, cover him with a blanket and push him out through the reception area under the noses of everyone. Outside, he would be loaded, wheelchair and all, into as 'Help the Aged' van full of old people. I hadn't a clue how they were going to get hold of the pensioners or what they would tell them. The idea was that everyone was going on a beano — a trip to the coast. The coach would travel to Dover and Ronnie would be switched on to a ship.

Once outside Europe, he would be flown to Margarita Island off the coast of Venezuela. It sounds incredible but, in the end, everything was set up, the charity bus was ready and, presumably, so were the old folk.

It was all a bit unreal for me. I did not know if it would work. Some of the crazy ventures that Ron got involved in never got past the first hurdle. This one was different. Things were happening — fast. Money changed hands at an alarming rate. It was all systems go.

Ron was taken into hospital. Security was tight, tighter than anyone had anticipated. He was held in a private room under guard 24 hours a day. The room was small with a tiny window. The sullen-faced guards who sat at the foot of Ron's bed made sure the curtains were always drawn. Two plain-clothed CID men were positioned outside. They tried hard to look inconspicuous, but failed miserably.

Mingling among other patients were undercover cops. They were easy to spot. They stood out like sore thumbs.

In the grounds surrounding the ward were even more police. At the entrance to the hospital were hundreds of Press all waiting to get a glimpse of Ronnie. The whole area was cordoned off. I wondered how the hell two fake American hospital porters were going to wheel Ronnie Kray out of the main entrance under the noses of this mob.

Someone was bound to recognise him, even if he was in a wheelchair with his knees covered by a red tartan blanket. The idea was ludicrous. The only people who were allowed to visit Ron in hospital were me and a couple of close friends.

The day of the operation came closer Ron became more and more paranoid. He was convinced there was a grass in the camp.

As D-Day arrived, everything was ready for the escape that would have rocked the nation. One of his friends and I went to visit Ron the day before his operation. When we got there, we were shocked. It wasn't Ron. He was like another person. Totally paranoid. He kept saying he smelt a rat.

We tried to reason with him, but the whole thing was making him ill — mentally. He was not happy and wanted to call it all off. I did try to pacify him by saying everything was all right, but Ron was having none of it.

I knew nothing I said was going to make any difference, especially when he was in that sort of mood. His friend tried to talk to him but still Ron was adamant.

'Call it off,' he snapped. 'Make the call.'

The guards looked up. I smiled. Ron scowled.

'Do as I say,' he demanded.

I left the hospital and rang his friends to say it was no go. Everything was on hold until after the operation. Maybe he would feel differently then.

The next day, Ron had his operation as planned. I went to see him and told him it still wasn't too late. He was adamant and refused to take any risks. He said he had a gut feeling something was wrong.

'Send the Yanks home,' he whispered. 'The plan is definitely off.'

It took Ron a few weeks to get over his paranoia, but I think calling the escape off was the best decision he ever made, because the police guard that day had been put on full alert and they were all wearing guns.

Maybe Ron was paranoid, but I think it was intuition.

6

Firm Friends

'Oh no. I can feel a Rene Wrigglesworth coming on.' That's what I say when someone wants to tell me all about their involvement with The Twins. Normally, it's not their own involvement that they are so keen to tell me about. It is nearly always some far-flung relative so far removed they can barely remember the person's name.

'Fred. No ... no ... wait a minute ... Frank. Big bloke. Looks like the robber's dog. You must know him?'

At this point, I just go along with them.

'Yeah ... yeah ... I know him. Wears a suit.'

It works every time. If only they realised that all gangsters wear suits.

They are adamant. 'That's him. That's the one. Knew you'd know him.'

It happens all over the country. The fact is, the Krays could never have had so many friends, relatives or associates if they had lived for 100 years.

The final straw came when a friend of mine, Freda, booked a holiday to Australia to see her brother, Peter. She had been chatting on the phone to him discussing arrangements about flights and all the places they were going to see. It came up in conversation that a friend of his, someone he had known for over 20 years, suddenly owned up to being related to the Kray twins.

I had never heard Ron talk about any family in Australia, so I asked what the name of this so-called relative down-under was supposed to be.

With a dead-pan expression, Freda replied, 'Rene Wrigglesworth ... I think.'

I fell about laughing. 'Rene fucking Wrigglesworth! You've got to be joking.'

Freda's face was a picture. 'No ... honest. I'm not,' she said in all innocence.

I just can't imagine someone called Rene Wrigglesworth being a member of the Kray family. So in my circle of close friends, it's now a standing joke that when someone starts saying that they know someone who knew the Krays, we call it 'Doing a Rene'.

Needless to say, the name was incorrect and Freda brought a photograph back from Australia of Rene. I must admit she does bear an uncanny resemblance to Ronnie. Maybe Rene is an exception to the rule and is related to him. Perhaps I will write to her one day — I will certainly send this book on to her, and hope she sees the funny side of it when we say 'Doing a Rene'. Even so, there are hundreds of people who claim to have met Ron, or at least saw him from afar. But there are not so many whom Ron would call friends, true friends.

Those are the ones who stood by him in the good times and the bad. Not fair-weather friends. Not the ones who wanted to visit him because he was Ronnie Kray. Not those who went just to boast later in the pub that they had been to visit him and that he was their friend. I'm not talking about those people. I'm talking about the people who really cared for him, and were there for him when the going got tough.

These were the people who sent him books, tobacco and toiletries, without being asked and more importantly, without expecting anything in return, some even spending their last few quid on him.

They say tough men don't cry. Well I've seen the toughest men in this country cry for Ronnie Kray because they cared for Ronnie Kray — the man — and not Ronnie Kray — the myth. This chapter is dedicated to them. The people that really matter. Ronnie Kray's 'firm friends'.

Joey Pyle

I met big Joey Pyle on the first visit I ever had with Ron. I had known Reggie for a while, and was nervous about meeting his brother, someone I had heard so much about. My first impression of Broadmoor, too, didn't exactly help to calm my nerves.

But having got through the security checks, and having broken the ice with Ron over a cup of tea and a few pleasantries, I was feeling a little more at ease. Ron was the perfect gentleman.

Then another man joined us — a big man in a big suit — and I got up to leave.

'No, don't go,' said Ron, and introduced me to his friend. Joey Pyle. The only man who consistently visited Ron every single week of his 28 years inside. Joey is an imposing man, someone you would be reluctant to approach without an introduction. His hair is black, slicked back, with grey around the sides, making him very distinguished. He has twinkling blue eyes that are soft with women and cold as ice around men.

I stood up and moved around the table so that Joe could sit next to Ron. Joe wanted to talk business. I sat back in my chair and tried not to listen but Ron wanted to include me in the conversation. He asked me to sit forward, not wanting to leave me out or make me feel uneasy.

I didn't have anything to say but Ron was always a gentleman and so aware of other people's feelings. He knew I would probably feel uncomfortable and went out of his way to put me at my ease.

When the visit had finished, Ron was taken out of the hall and turned to the left. Joe and I were escorted out and went to the right. I looked over my shoulder and noticed that Ron had stopped. He was watching me and Joe being led along the corridor. Joe put his arm around my shoulder. He turned round, smiled, and winked at Ron.

'See you later, Colonel,' he said with a saucy grin.

Ron folded his arms and smiled, too. He knew exactly what Joe was doing — teasing him.

That was in 1987. From that day on, Joey became my friend as well. Joey has always been a good business man and a man of his word. Ron told me once that when Joey Pyle gave his word, it might just as well be written in stone. Ron trusted Joey with his life.

Whenever there was a party that I had to attend, it was always Joey and his close friends whom Ron trusted to escort me. It was at these parties that I met all of Ron's firm friends.

When I decided to write this chapter, I knew that Joey Pyle would be first on my list. I phoned Joey but, before he agreed to take part, he wanted to know what the book was called and, more importantly, what it was about. After I explained, he was more than happy to contribute.

This is what Joey said:

I knew as soon as I met Ronnie Kray he was something special and we became friends almost straight away.

It was way back in the '50s when I met him. We were only in our 20s but Ron was already a man to know. His fearsome reputation preceded him, but he was also known for his sincerity and his loyalty.

Indeed, if you made a friend of Ronnie Kray, you made a friend for life. If, on the other hand, you made an enemy of him, you paid the ultimate price. I got on all right with him, we had something in common — boxing. Initially, it was this that brought us together. We were the same age and mixed in the same circles. I went on to became a professional middleweight fighter. Ron loved boxing. He was good at it, too. So was Reggie.

Ron could have gone a long way in the boxing world, but he didn't have the discipline that boxing demanded. He had other ideas. Big ideas. He wanted to get to the top. He didn't have time for early morning jogs and workouts. He was far too impatient.

During the '50s and '60s we were always bumping into each other. I often had a drink with him in the Astor Club just off Berkeley Square. He had been off doing his bit of business and I had been doing mine.

The Astor Club was the place to go when all the pubs were closed, therefore it was usually in the early hours of the morning that we started doing the odd bit of business together, which meant I would regularly have a drink with Reg and Ron in the East End, which was their manor. In return, they would come over to the West End to return the compliment.

Ron and I shared the same passion — good suits and monogrammed shirts. The night my son was born, Joey Junior, we had a huge party in the Astor Club. It was a night to remember.

Joey Pyle has just come out of prison after doing six years for drug smuggling. The day Joey was sentenced, Ron said that he felt that that was the last time he would ever see Joey. I tried to reassure him. But he was adamant. I don't know how he knew he just did. Ron was psychic like that.

After Joey was sentenced, obviously he was no longer able to visit Ronnie, but his incarceration didn't stop him from writing. I know for a fact that they wrote to each other every week.

When Ron died, Joey was devastated. Because Joey was Category 'A' he wasn't allowed to attend Ron's funeral. I knew how Joey would be feeling. He was Ronnie's closest friend and wanted to show his respects and couldn't. It was obvious he would feel left out.

Because I knew what Ronnie meant to Joey, I wanted to include him in some way. I noticed on the service sheet that Joey's name had been included in the names of people who were not able to attend. I thought Joey might like a copy of the service sheet, but they were as rare as rocking-horse shit.

On the day of the funeral sightseers were offering hundreds of pounds for a copy, especially one with the Kray name printed on it.

So, after the funeral, I photocopied my service sheet and I sent it to Joey. A few days later, a letter arrived from Joey thanking me. Attached to the letter was a poem.

In the letter Joey explained that whilst he had been locked up in his cell, he felt Ron's presence and felt compelled to write the poem.

I do believe Joey, when he said that Ron came to him that night in his cell. Maybe Ron had something on his mind. Maybe he just wanted to say goodbye. Joey has never written a poem before or since; Ron, on the other hand, has had poems published.

The words in the poem are quite poignant. Joey says they're Ron's words, not his. I think it is beautiful.

The time has come to say my farewell
But there's a few things I'd like to tell
For 26 years they've kept me confined
They said I was mad and out of my mind
I never let my pals down, and I went with the
  grain
If that's being mad, then I must be insane
I've done some bad things and I've done some good
But I always did good before bad, if I could
I was deprived of my freedom for so many years
But feel no pity, and don't shed tears
As I'm free from the screws and that stinking cell
Free from the slop-outs, and that Broadmoor hell
So feel no sadness, and please don't mourn
For I haven't left you, I'm just reborn
So Kate remember, I'm a whisper away
And we'll get it together again some day ...

Every time I read this I get goose-bumps. I really do believe that it was a message from Ron and so did Joey. I feel strangely comforted by the poem.

After a lifetime of fighting with madness and 26 years of imprisonment, Ronnie is finally free and at peace. One of the things I asked Joey, while I was interviewing him, was what made Ron special to him.

Joey's a man of few words. His voice broke as he struggled say, 'Ronnie Kray was "a Man" — and there will never be another one like him.'

Laurie O'Leary

Another person who was close to Ron and had been since Ronnie was ten years old is a man called Laurie O'Leary. The first time I met Laurie was at my wedding reception at The Hilton Hotel, Bracknell, Berkshire, in 1989. Although I had spoken to him many times on the phone, I had never actually met him in person until then. Laurie's a big man, well groomed and wears fashionable clothes that make him look younger than his years. He is a good-looking man, very friendly, but stands no nonsense from anyone. He used to be Doris Stoke's manager, and his brother Alfie was once Eric Clapton's minder. He's always been a good friend to me, too, and I love him very much. He is probably the nicest man I've ever met, a real character, and I know Laurie won't mind me saying this, but he can also talk the hind leg off a donkey!

Laurie was one of the last people to see Ron alive. He went and saw Ron on a visit two weeks before he died. Ron asked him to write a book to put the record straight about all the crap that had previously been written about him. In my opinion, Laurie O'Leary is the only man from the old days who could undertake such a task. He has probably forgotten more stories about Ronnie Kray than most people could ever have known.

He knows stories from ages ago when Ronnie was a young, impetuous boy, from the time when he had tuberculosis until the day he died. He is a mine of information.

At the moment, Laurie is in the throws of writing his own book, so I felt a bit apprehensive about asking him to contribute to mine. Maybe, just maybe, he might say 'No'. and maybe he might blank me.

But Laurie is such a nice man, he had no hesitation in helping me with the information I needed. Indeed, he was only too happy to be involved. This is what he said:

The Colonel. You have to have known the man to understand him. He was a powerful man. A man that could not stand bullies. I knew him for nearly 50 years and never saw him duck away from anybody. I have read many stories in the newspapers, and I've heard mugs say that he ducked out of situations. Ronnie Kray never ducked out of fuck all. Nothing. Sure, he beat up bullies. But he wasn't a bully himself.

Only a few weeks before he died, I went to see him in the hospital. He was very ill at that time but we started chatting about this and that. Eventually the subject got around to bullies. I said, 'You hate bullies, Ron, don't you?'

Ronnie glared at me. He had completely misheard what I had said. He thought I had said that he was a bully. Quickly, I explained that I said that he hated bullies. He growled, 'Yes I do ... bastards.'

Even though he was so ill, he couldn't control his feelings towards bullies. He hated any sort of bullying, be it verbal or anything else. He always stuck up for the underdog. That was his nature.

I met Ronnie Kray when I was 10 years old, which is over 50 years ago. Ronnie was my mate, the best mate I've ever had or am ever likely to have.

I lived in the next street to the twins and we all grew up together. Ronnie encouraged me to box and, at times, we used to go road running together.

We were good mates. Later on, when he had taken over a few clubs, Ronnie asked me to run this dance club for him below a casino. That was back in 1962. Then I went into running a swish club that was owned by George Harrison, one of The Beatles. They were the real days. The Swinging Sixties and, boy, did we swing.

I've always been around The Twins. It was fun to be around them. Dangerous, but fun. The only time I had a break from seeing Ronnie was when he was first sentenced. I didn't see him for nearly four years because villains were not allowed to visit other villains. Not that I am a villain, because I'm not. I have always been legit, but I think that the authorities thought that anyone connected with the twins at that time was a villain. It wasn't until Ronnie was transferred to Parkhurst on the Isle of Wight that I was eventually allowed to see him.

It was at Parkhurst that Ronnie became paranoid. When his mum and I visited him, he was in such a state, it was obvious he was mentally disturbed. I hardly recognised him. When he was eventually transferred to Broadmoor, I think everyone was relieved. At least in a hospital he would get the proper medication that he needed.

It was a relief, especially for his mum, Violet. She was a lovely lady. Salt of the earth. The epitome of a loving mum and, one thing's for sure, she absolutely idolised Ron.

One of the things that is not well known about Ron was his sense of humour. Without knowing it, he was an extremely funny man. It was his dry wit and one-liners that had me in tears of laughter on more than one occasion.

Years ago, I used to manage the world-famous

clairvoyant called Doris Stokes. She was brilliant and just blew my mind. Ronnie was psychic himself and was very interested in seeing Doris Stokes on a visit. We made the long journey to Broadmoor to see Ronnie. As usual, he was dressed immaculately. I introduced her to him. 'Doris, this is Ronnie Kray.'

He held her hand gently and smiled. Ron was such a polite man. He took her coat and pulled the chair out for her to sit down.

'Here you are, Mrs Stokes,' he said.

It was obvious from the start that she was smitten with him.

'Oh ... you can call me Doris,' she cooed.

'Well then, you can call me Ron,' he replied. 'Would you like a pork pie or smoked salmon sandwich?'

I couldn't believe what he had just asked her. A fucking pork pie? Smoked salmon sandwich?

I think poor old Doris was in shock.

'No, I'll just have a cup of tea,' she mumbled.

Another one of Ron's visitors arrived. He was a writer and had come to talk business. We all settled down around the tea-stained table, each taking turns to talk to Ron.

Suddenly, Doris said, 'I've got your mum here with me, Ron.'

Ronnie looked at her in amazement and said, 'But Doris, my mother's dead.'

The writer and I looked at each other not knowing what to say and more importantly, trying not to laugh. Sensing my stifled laughter, Ronnie leant over and whispered in my ear, 'I think Doris should be in here, Laurie, and I should be out there.'

I could contain my laughter no longer. Both Ron and I burst out with a raucous laugh.

That day, and that visit with the writer and Doris Stokes, was a memorable one for me. We all enjoyed it so much and Doris couldn't get over what a gentleman Ron was.

The last thing Ron asked me was, 'Do you believed in life after death?'

I told him, 'Yes, I do, Ron, and you only meet nice people on the other side, not evil people.'

Ron paused, took a deep breath, dragged on his fag and smiled.

'Thank fuck for that, Laurie,' he replied.

Charlie Walker

Charlie Walker is a man of his word. He is a proud man, and one I am proud to have as my friend. He has an air of confidence about him and you know instantly it wouldn't be wise to cross him.

He is a big, broad man and knows how to act with everyone. He is always 'suit to boot' and cuts a dash. When Charlie Walker is present, you are immediately aware of him because he stands out as an immovable object

It was in the summer of 1988 when Ron asked me to phone Charlie to arrange a visit. He was such a friendly man that we clicked immediately. In those early days, I have to put my hands up and admit that I was green and didn't know the score. I was always eager to please Ron. I tried to do all the things he wanted but it was impossible.

There was always so much to do. So many messages to deliver, so many people to see and places to go. It seemed that Ron had completely taken over my life and there was no time left for me any more.

Charlie sensed that and encouraged me to slow down. I am pleased to say that I took his advice and, since then, he has phoned me every week without fail, not for anything in particular, just to see if things are OK and if I need anything.

He loved Ronnie Kray, that was obvious, and when Ron died he was devastated. The last time I saw Charlie was when I was paying my last respects to Ron at the funeral parlour which was under siege by TV crews, journalists from all over the world and thousands of fans all wanting to see Ron for the last time. Grim-looking men with broken noses and wearing cashmere overcoats surrounded the Chapel of Rest.

Reggie had control of who was allowed in and who wasn't. He had made a list of names in order of priority.

Obviously, Reggie went first to pay his respects. Charlie Kray was second on the list, and I was third. Unless your name was on that list, you could forget it.

Charlie Walker arrived while I was with Ron. I had so much I wanted to tell Ron, but a gentle knock on the door broke my thoughts.

'Sorry to disturb you, Kate, but there is a man at the door called Charlie Walker. He said you know him.'

I was so pleased that it was Charlie; I needed to see a familiar face.

Charlie was shown into the Chapel of Rest. He looked pale and drawn it was obvious he had been crying but he managed to keep his grief under control. He put his arms around me and hugged me tight. His huge arms engulfed me. It was a great comfort. Slowly, he peered into the oak coffin, the brass handles shining in the sunlight coming through the window.

Flowers, mainly spring flowers, were everywhere and their scent filled the air. Ron's body looked like a cold marble statue. Charlie bent forward and gently kissed Ron's forehead. Tears welled up in his eyes, and there was genuine pain etched on his tough face, a face that had seen many a brawl in its day. Finally, he broke down and cried.

I didn't know how to comfort him. I just didn't have the words. It nearly broke my heart. I've heard it said that tough men don't cry. Well that day, I saw a tough man cry for his friend. The man he describes as 'a diamond'.

This is Charlie Walker's story:

The phone rang. I peered at my alarm clock. It was seven o'clock in the morning. I rubbed my eyes.

'The Twins have been nicked.'

I didn't understand what the caller was saying, but the urgency in his voice startled me.

'Who the fuck's talking?' I snapped.

'Charlie, it's Checa Berry, the twins have been nicked. It's serious. Get dressed, I'll be around in ten minutes.'

He explained that there had been a dawn raid and that Reg and Ron had been nicked. I couldn't believe it. Not an hour earlier we had been mob-handed in the Astor Club having a good knees-up.

I had driven Ron home about six o'clock that morning and dropped him off at Braithwaite House where Ron had a flat. Thinking back on it now, there was a heavy police presence that night around the East End. Police cars were parked everywhere.

I said to Ron, 'Something's going down,' and I asked him whether I should drive around the back roads . But Ron was riding high.

'Fuck 'em,' he laughed. 'They're all mugs.'

We all roared with laughter. I wonder if we would have laughed so loud if we had realised that that night and, in particular, that party at the Astor Club, was to be Ronnie Kray's last night of freedom.

It was through two brothers called Checa and Teddy Berry that I met the Krays. I was a friend of Teddy and Checa's. They were two tough bastards that didn't like The Twins. It was inevitable that the brothers would end up having a row.

And, boy, did they have a row. Ron went right 'into one' and shot Teddy in the leg. The wound turned bad and Teddy had to have his leg amputated. Ron felt terrible about it because the row was over something stupid and certainly didn't warrant someone losing their leg.

Ron just lost his temper. The twins tried to put things straight by arranging a big party for Teddy at the York Hall in the East End of London.

It was a marvellous evening, everyone that was anyone attended. Ronnie made sure of that. They raised enough money to buy Teddy a pub called the Bridge House, off Bow Common Lane. Checa and Teddy took over the pub and were good hosts and it was a roaring success.

For a while, things quietened down between Teddy and Ron. But, deep down, the Berry brothers still resented The Twins, Ronnie in particular.

They barred them from their pub because of the shooting. Well, I say barred them. Let's just say they made it known that they were not welcome to go in their pub. I suppose it was understandable under the circumstances. I didn't really know the twins at that time. Sure, I'd seen them around and I knew of them, everybody did. You would of had to come from another planet not to have heard of them.

Then, one night, right out of the blue, Teddy changed his mind and said that the twins could come to the pub, and they would be made welcome. The Bridge House was my local. I always drunk there. When the twins eventually visited the pub, it was as if nothing had happened. Everybody was friends again. That kind of thing often happened and you never knew what had gone on behind the scenes.

So that's where I met them, in Teddy and Checa's pub. I got on brilliantly with the twins, especially Ron. He *gave me the job of running John Pearson around. He was the writer that wrote the best-selling book* Professions of Violence. *That was the first book ever written about the twins; it was in their heyday at the height of their professional career.*

The very fact that someone wanted to write a book about them that might turn them into instant celebrities pleased them immensely.

The twins let Pearson shadow them around everywhere, even putting him up in a flat in Bethnal Green and paying for minders to drive him to all the clubs. I was one of those minders.

When the book was eventually released, Ron hated what Pearson had written. That aside, it did prove to be a good source of income for them for many years. Ron still got a pension out of that book right up until his death.

I'm glad Ron didn't die in Broadmoor. At least he was spared the indignity of dying in prison. Broadmoor's gone mad since Ron's been gone.

Peter Sutcliffe, the Yorkshire Ripper, has been blinded in one eye. Ian Kay, another inmate, stabbed him in both eyes with a felt-tipped pen. Sutcliffe was on the same ward as Ron, in the very next cell. The stabbing would never have happened if Ron was still there; he just wouldn't have allowed it. Sutcliffe wants a glass eye but Broadmoor has refused on the grounds that he could smash it up and use all the little bits of glass to cut his own wrists or cut someone else. Sounds crazy, but plausible, given the nutcases that are there.

I don't wish Ronnie back in Broadmoor, not for one minute. There is nothing I would have loved more than to see him back in the East End having a drink with his friends.

For me, when Ronnie died, it was the end of an era. The end of the Swinging Sixties. End of the gangsters.

End of the good life. My Life. It's just not the same any more. When Ronnie Kray died, a big part of me died with him.

Roy Shaw

Roy Shaw is probably the meanest-looking man I have ever seen in the whole of my life. His face, in particular his nose, looks like it's been broken more times than a bone china teacup. His cold, expressionless eyes look like they belong to a great white man-eating shark. However, this doesn't detract from his good looks. He is not very tall, about 5ft 8in, but he is as wide as he is short and always impeccably dressed. His hands are as big as a bunch of bananas with a grip like a set of Stillsons. You have never come across a smarter man than Roy Shaw.

The first time I met him was again at my wedding reception in Crowthorne, Berkshire. He was there with Joey Pyle's men. Roy was a bare-knuckle fighter. He fought Lenny Maclean, another of Ron's good friends. The two champions are an awesome sight and it is impossible to tell them apart as far as strength goes.

But Roy Shaw is one mean bastard. If you cross him, you are either incredibly stupid or incredibly brave.

I phoned Roy and asked him if he wanted to be involved in the book. His response shocked me. He was really pleased that I had phoned him. He said it was an honour to be in a book about Ron. More importantly, he thought it was an honour to be one of Ron's friends.

When he first answered the telephone, he

growled. I thought he had been asleep. I said, 'Sorry, Roy, were you asleep?'

'No, I always talk like this,' he said.

I laughed. So did Roy. Thank God!

I wasn't sure how or when he met Ron. All I knew is that Ron liked him and respected him. I asked Roy how he met Ron. This is 'Big Roy' Shaw's story:

Ronnie came to visit me in Broadmoor three times in all in 1963. I was doing time — a long time. Someone had told me that if you get transferred to Broadmoor it's a lot easier. You get more visits, better food, in all it's more of a relaxed régime. Better still, when the doctors think they have cured you, they send you to a normal hospital and eventually home. It's generally known that it's a quicker and simpler way of doing your time. It's called 'working your ticket'.

I was really violent. I knocked out every screw that got in my way. I did time in some of the toughest nicks in Britain. In the end, there was no place that was prepared to take me. There was only one place left — Broadmoor.

Ronnie Kray came to see me there long before he was sentenced to life. He came with Ronnie Hart, his cousin, the cousin that was later to become his betrayer. When he visited me in Broadmoor Hospital, I was having a few problems. My main problem was with my wife.

I suspected that she was messing about with another man, having an affair. Ronnie asked me if there was anything he could do. I told him about my wife. I said that I wanted the man hurt — hurt bad. Ron didn't hesitate.

'Consider it done,' he said. 'Don't worry about nothing, Roy, I'll take care of it.'

Ron came to see me a few days later. He was true to

his word. Quietly he whispered, 'It's done. He's been shot.'

From that day on, I have always had the utmost respect for the man. If Ronnie Kray said that he would do something, you knew he would do it. He was a man of his word.

When I was first in Broadmoor and Ronnie came to visit me, I can honestly say that I didn't know that he was gay. He was such a man's man. We were on a visit and Ronnie asked me what it was like in Broadmoor.

'It's not bad, not bad at all,' I told him. 'There is only one drawback. It's full of poofs.'

Ronnie's eyes lit up. 'Is it, Roy? That's smashin'.'

Jack Lee

Jack Lee doesn't look like a gangster, he looks like a bank manager. Just an ordinary, everyday man you might pass in the street without a sideways glance, but behind this ordinary 'Joe' is a hidden past spanning 30 years. There isn't anything going on in the East End that he doesn't know about; he makes it his business to know. Jack Lee is the epitome of a loveable rogue. He is full of amusing stories and anecdotes and his sense of humour is renowned. He was a good friend to Ron over the years and was extremely kind and generous to him.

This is Jack Lee's story:

It was like a rugby scrum. We put our heads together. Our eyes met. Nobody said a word. Four top-ranking gang members meeting around a Formica-topped table in a hospital for the criminally insane. The meeting in Broadmoor had been called by the heads of all the different gangs that controlled London. I had never seen anything like it. Who was going to break the silence and speak first? Our eyes narrowed and we all glared at each other. It could only have been for a few seconds but seemed forever. Ron's face softened and a cheeky grin spread across his face. In an instant we all burst out laughing. Once we started laughing we couldn't stop. We went from cool professional businessmen to delinquent schoolboys. If a newspaper journalist had been a fly on the wall they would never have believed it.

All four gang leaders laughing like children.

There was only one Ronnie Kray. He was such a complex character. He was probably the most genuine man I have ever met. If I took anyone to visit him, I used to pre-warn them not to compliment Ron on any of his jewellery. If they did, he would take that jewellery off and give it to them. It didn't matter what it was. Watch, cuff-links, diamond ring; if you complimented him on it, he would give it away. That's what he was like.

I have never known a man to give away as many watches as he did. But you never really knew where you stood with him. One day he would give you a five grand gold and diamond watch, the next day he would call you a 'slag and a rat'. I never took that to heart because you wasn't anyone to Ronnie Kray unless, at one time or another, he had called you a 'slag and a rat'.

I cannot say he used that phrase as a term of endearment. At the time he called you it, he fucking meant it. But that time soon passed. The following week I'd be back up on a visit, laughing and joking with him. Only Ronnie Kray had the charisma that allowed him to do that. I miss him. There will never be another man like him.

Mickey Chambers

Alias 'Cornish' Mick. He is called that for the obvious reason — he comes from Cornwall. I met 'Cornish' through Joey Pyle. Whenever I went to any parties it was always Joey Pyle, Ronnie Fields and 'Cornish Mick' who escorted me. I couldn't have been in safer hands.

'Cornish' Mick is of slight build. He reminds me of a typical dad, one who would push the kids on a swing or mow the lawn on a Sunday afternoon. But 'Cornish' Mick is, without a doubt, one dangerous 'mother-fucker'. He is a ladies' man, a real wow with the girls. His young wife, Linda, doesn't take any notice of his fraternisations. When Mick phones me he always tells me he loves me, and I hear Linda laughing in the background, saying, 'You must be talking to Kate Kray. I can hear him Kate ...'

I am proud to have Mickey 'Cornish' as my friend. He was a good friend to Ron and he is someone who would never let me down. It would not matter whose company he is in. If anybody was rude to me, 'Cornish' would stop them dead.

In this dog-eat-dog world — the underworld — sometimes you are in favour and sometimes you are not. Some are quick to jump on the band wagon and take any opportunity to slag you off. That's exactly what happened to me. Some people, some that I have never met and some I have, think that I had ulterior motives for marrying Ron. It was for money;

it was for the name; it was for the fame. I've heard them all. It doesn't bother me. People are all entitled to their own opinions and when things started to go wrong between me and Ron, those same people started to slag me off, foolishly thinking they might curry favour with Ron.

They were wrong, because Ron never turned his back on me. His real friends knew that would never happen. Only the mugs thought that he would.

But at certain functions, certain people felt they knew all along that I was a 'wrong un' and had to voice their opinions. But not in 'Cornish' Mick's company they didn't.

Mick was happy be in this book. This is his story:

'Do you know Katie? Have you ever met her?'

The answers are always the same.

'No. No.'

'Then shut your foul mouth.'

I wouldn't have anyone say a bad word about Katie Kray. And I want everybody to know it. She is a good girl. If Ronnie Kray didn't marry her as quick as he did, then I would have stolen her for myself!

Not the sort of thing that anyone would say to Ronnie Kray, but I did, although I'm glad he saw the funny side of it.

We were all on a visit with him. There was Joe, Ronnie Fields, Ronnie Kray, Katie Kray and me. They hadn't been married long. We got all the relevant business out of the way and was sitting around chatting. Ron was teasing Kate, saying how at the tender age of 33 she was a little bit too old for him.

Maybe he would trade her in for a new model. It was funny because he was 23 years older than her. Katie was laughing. We all were.

I turned to Ron and said, 'If you don't want her, I'll be

more than happy to take her off your hands.'

The conversation stopped dead. You could have heard a pin drop. For a moment, Ron glared at me. One of those glares. Then a broad grin spread across his face. From that day, Ronnie Kray knew how I felt about his wife. She was good for him. She made him laugh. She brought happiness to him in that God-forsaken place, Broadmoor.

God knows he could do with a little happiness after being locked up for 26 years. Thirty years for the crime he committed was a diabolical liberty. In all the years I visited Ronnie Kray, I never heard him complain — not once.

'Don't worry about me. Get Reggie out.' That was his main concern. His priority was to get Reg out. But that was him. Always thinking about other people and never himself.

Tony Lambrianou

Tony Lambrianou was sentenced to life imprisonment at the Old Bailey in 1968. He stood in the dock side by side with Ron. He did 15 years for his part in disposing of Jack the Hat's body. He didn't grass. When he got life, he was 25 years old. He didn't complain — not once.

I met Tony on a visit with Ron. He is a big imposing man with silver-grey hair, looking every bit the gangster. The first thing that strikes you about Tony is his distinctive voice. It is deep and demanding. If he said 'sit', everyone would obey, not just the dog. He has a menacing look, with eyes that hold you and you would be a fool to cross him. He spent 15 years in some of the toughest prisons in Britain, and he never betrayed Ron.

Ron told me that I could always trust Tony, that he was a loyal friend. Since his release from prison, he has written a best-selling book called *Inside the Firm*. It has just been released in London as a play. I'm glad for him. He deserves every success.

These are Tony's memories of Ron:

John Pearson approached the twins to write the book Professions of Violence *in 1968. We had a meeting one day in Teddy Berry's pub just off Bethnal Green Road. Ronnie said that John Pearson was coming to the East End to see him and that he was going to write his autobiography. Ronnie wanted to put on a show for him and arranged for a few of the boys to be in the bar 'suited up' looking the part.*

We all sat around drinking beer, waiting for Pearson to show up. Ron was in a great mood. Half-an-hour later, John Pearson arrived. He desperately wanted to fit in with us boys. He walked in or, should I say, swaggered in. We looked at each other, then looked at him in amazement. Boy did he have some nerve. He winked at us and waved.

'All right boys?'

We laughed. So did Ron.

He got himself a drink, sat down at our table and started to talk. He liked the sound of his own voice and was going on and on about how he wanted to live in the East End, how much he loved the place and all the friendly people that lived there. What a mug. He was just trying to be one of the boys. We weren't silly. We could see straight through him. We just went along with him. Unbeknown to him, Ronnie had him sussed. He had things all lined up for the unsuspecting Mr Pearson.

Ron had a little flat just off Vallance Road. He called it the dungeon. It was a dingy little place in an old tenement building. It was a right dump — disgusting. The roof leaked and it was damp and cold. There were no carpets on the floor and an old black-and-white television stood on a wooden crate in the corner.

The wallpaper, what was left of it, looked as though it had been put up in the war. The place was running alive with cockroaches as big as armadillos. Ronnie had it as a hideaway. We used to have parties there. Drinking parties.

Ronnie laughed. 'So he wants a taste of the fucking East End does he? I'll stick him in the dungeon. That will sort him out.'

Poor old Pearson. He had to stay in that rat-hole for over a month. Worst of all, he had to pretend to Ronnie that he loved it. Ron enjoyed making him squirm. He kept asking, 'How you getting on in that flat, John?'

We all knew that he hated it. Through gritted teeth he

answered every time

'Oh, lovely, Ron. Just lovely.'

He was sick. Sick as a dog. We are talking about John Pearson. The John Pearson that wrote Ian Flemming's life story. In those days, it was a big thing to be a writer. Ronnie didn't give a fuck who he was. He wound him up mercilessly.

Pearson broke in the end. 'Do you know what, Tony?' he said. 'I hate that fucking flat.'

I'll never forget the look on his face. I didn't have the heart to tell him that Ronnie was winding him up. I bet to this day he still remembers the dungeon.

Only Ronnie Kray could get away with something like that.

I have a million stories about Ron. His sense of humour was second to none.

When Checa Berry knew that The Twins were coming to drink in his pub, he would push the boat out. Anyone would think royalty was coming. He would do plates of sandwiches, have minders on the door, the whole bit.

One day, I noticed that beside the till they kept a big glass jar full of little lead pellets. I called Checa over and asked him what they were.

'Fucking shotgun pellets, that's what they are,' he snapped.

He explained that his pub was shot up that often, the whole of the bar was peppered with these little lead pellets. Once they're lodged in the wall, they're a bugger to get out.'

Now and again, much to Checa's annoyance, one or two of them would work loose and fall on the floor. Every day Checa would go around muttering to himself as he picked the little pellets up and put them in the glass jar.

One night, Ronnie laughed and said, 'I don't know why he picks them up. It's a waste of time. He will be picking them up all his fucking life.'

Ronnie did like a shoot-up. He loved guns. Years later when he was in Broadmoor he still never lost his fascination for them.

I took a man into Broadmoor to visit Ronnie. His name was Bill. He came out of Romford. Like Ronnie, Bill had a thing about guns. He loved them and sold them. That was his business, or so he said.

I took him up to Broadmoor to meet Ron as I knew that they would get on. More to the point, I knew Ron would find him useful. On the visit, Bill made a fatal mistake. He told Ron that he had a Thompson sub-machine-gun and that he could get Ron any gun he wanted.

'Just say the word,' he bragged.

Ron listened intently, but said nothing. I knew he wouldn't say nothing for long.

A few days later, my phone rang. It was Ron. 'Get that Bill up on a visit again,' he said.

I laughed. I knew that when Ronnie wanted to see a stranger on a second visit, it could only mean one thing. He had thought about it and had now got a use for him.

I made all the arrangements. The visit was booked for first thing the next morning. When we arrived to see Ronnie, he was dressed impeccably — as usual.

Bill and I ordered our tea from the waiter. Ron ordered his usual, non-alcoholic lager. It was obvious that he had something on his mind. We didn't have to wait long to find out what it was. He held Bill's arm and pulled him close so nobody could overhear what he was about to say.

'When I get out,' he whispered, 'can I loan your machine-gun? You see, I still have some unfinished business.'

Bill was stunned. He didn't know what to say. He had visited Ronnie acting the big man. Talking big. To Bill it was just a fantasy. To Ronnie it was stark reality.

Ron said to me once, 'Never forget what they did to us. Never trust anyone.'

By that, he meant the bastards that betrayed us. I will never forget those words from Ronnie. They are wise words. He made the mistake of trusting certain people and it got him 30 years. Me, too. I trusted the same people and got 15 years. I, too, will never forget what they did to us. To use Ronnie Kray's own words, they are 'slags and rats'. You have to respect the man. Ronnie Kray demanded respect.

I always came away from Broadmoor after visiting Ron feeling very depressed. The reason was, I always used to tell Ronnie that, one day, he would be free. I wanted to believe that, but in my heart I knew that was never going to happen.

We were all sentenced at the Old Bailey together. I did 15 years. I was the first one of the lifers to get out. Ronnie Kray was delighted. He was genuinely delighted. In the 26 years that Ron spent in prison I never heard him complain. I also never heard him talk about being free. I found that sad.

Albert Reading

I met Albert Reading on a secret rendezvous on the South Circular in a shop called The World of Leather.

Ron had asked me to ring Albert to arrange a meeting with him to discuss some business they were doing at the time. I didn't know what he looked like or how I was going to recognise him, but that was not a problem as I had been in that position many times before. I walked into that shop on a Saturday afternoon not fully prepred for what was going to happen.

I looked around the half-empty shop, carefully studying potential buyers. There was a fat man wearing a pair of striped shorts. He had a small child on his shoulders who was eating an ice cream. Nah ... that wasn't him. A yuppie brushed past me wearing a cheap suit and holding a filofax, talking on his mobile phone. Nah ... that wasn't him either.

I stood in the middle of the shop gazing around; the smell of the leather was overwhelming. I wondered where the hell he was. Then, from out of nowhere, a swivel chair spun round. The man in the chair was striking. He wore a silver-grey suit with a tightly knotted silk tie. His rugged face was tanned, and his jet-black hair, slightly greying at the sides, gave him a distinguished look. He oozed money, power and sex appeal. It was Albert Reading.

He leaned back in the chair nonchalantly,

seemingly without a care for anyone or anything. He smiled. I remember thinking how handsome he was, a very distinctive man, his appearance giving nothing away about his chequered past.

Albert has spent 36 years in prison, his last sentence was a 25-year stretch for armed robbery. He has had the birch. He has been stabbed, shot, beaten, but he is the most personable and generous man you could wish to meet. Instantly, we clicked.

This is Albert Reading's story:

I met the twins in Stepney, initially through boxing. My dad was a professional fighter and the twins used to visit him — he would talk to them about boxing for hours. We were all called up to the Army together and were billeted to Colchester barracks. The Sergeant Major took an instant dislike to us. He thought he could shout at us and order us about. He was wrong. He was soon to experience the wrath of Ronnie Kray.

When the post was distributed, the Sergeant Major yelled out your name.

'... READING ... KRAY ...'

If there was a letter for you, he tossed it at you like skimming a pebble across a pond. This particular day, Ronnie received a letter from his mother.

'KRAY,' the Sergeant Major yelled, then he skimmed the letter in Ron's direction.

The letter flew through the air as if in slow motion and landed in front of Ronnie's shiny boots. Ron's eyes narrowed. He looked straight into the Sergeant Major's eyes. Every one of us knew that look. It was the look of trouble. Ron motioned to the letter on the floor.

'Pick it up,' he growled.

For someone to speak to the Sergeant Major in such a manner was unheard of.

'Pick my mother's letter up,' Ron whispered again.

The Sergeant Major looked dumbfounded, but stood his ground and bellowed, 'YOU WHAT, YOU 'ORRIBLE LITTLE MAN?'

Ron's eyes were as black as thunder. He glared at the Sergeant Major. 'You heard what I said. Pick it up.'

Ron never raised his voice. He never took his eyes off his adversary. Their eyes were locked and it was a battle of wills. There was no way Ron was going to back down; his face said it all. The Sergeant Major sensed trouble — big trouble. He looked away from Ron's piercing gaze. Slowly, not making any sudden moves, he bent down and picked up the letter and submissively handed it to Ron.

For his insolence, Ron was sent to the choky, but it didn't bother him — he was a man of principle. If he felt strongly enough about something, the consequences were irrelevant. I loved Ron's ways, his manner. He wasn't mouthy, he was a man of his word. I had the utmost respect for him.

Billy Murray

Billy Murray and Ronnie Kray go back a long way. Billy is an actor — a bloody good actor, too. He has been in many films and in countless TV programmes. At present, he is in the popular Thames Television programme *The Bill*, in which he plays DS Don Beech.

Ron phoned me and wanted to see me on a visit urgently. There was nothing unusual in that. He always wanted to see me and it was always urgent. As usual, I made the long journey to Broadmoor. Ron was waiting for me. He always looked smart, but on this particular day he was dressed immaculately. We sat down at the small table in the crowded visiting hall. Ron explained that he was expecting another visitor, a special visitor. His name was Billy Murray.

'You'll like Billy,' Ron smirked. 'You wait 'til you see him, he's handsome.'

Ron has said that before but his idea of handsome was certainly not mine. So I just smiled sweetly at him and nodded. Ron didn't take a blind bit of notice of me as he was far too busy talking about Billy. He went on to say that a few of The Firm went to Barcelona back in the 1960s and Billy went with them.

'Was he one of your boys?' I asked.

Ron looked disappointed and frowned. 'Billy Murray was the only man that got away from me. We were only friends, unfortunately.'

I was suprised. Ron always got what he wanted, but not Billy Murray.

Ron went on to say, 'You'd be surprised ... the "faces" that didn't get away from me, but some secrets are best left untold.'

However, on this occasion, I had to agree with Ron. Billy Murray is indeed handsome. I'd even go so far as to say he is drop-dead gorgeous. It didn't make any difference to Ron that Billy never became one of his boys because he thought Billy was a really nice person, and if he couldn't have him as one of his boys then he wanted him as a friend. That was back in the 1960s. They remained friends until the day Ron died in 1995.

Harry Roberts

In 1965, Harry Roberts was Britain's most wanted man.

On Friday, 12 August, in a quiet street near London's Shepherd's Bush, he and two accomplices gunned down three policemen.

Until then, the murder of a British policeman was virtually unheard of. To most people, it was the kind of thing you only saw in Hollywood gangster movies. The crime, and the front-page photographs of three bloodied policemen lying dead in the street, shocked the country.

Two of the killers — John Duddy and Jack Whitney — were arrested within a week, but it was three long months before the police caught up with Harry Roberts.

In 1966, at the end of his trial, Mr Justice Glynn Jones described the murders as 'perhaps the most heinous crimes to have been committed in this country for a generation or more.' He sent Harry Roberts to prison for life with a recommendation that he serve at least 30 years.

I first met Harry in Gartree High Security Prison in the late 1980s. By then he had served over 20 years. Later, I wrote Harry's story in my book *Lifers*. It was the first time he had told his story to anyone. Since then we have become friends, and he phones me from prison every week.

I asked him if he wanted to contribute to this book, and he was more than happy to give his opinion of Ron. In the next post I received a letter from Harry. His letters are always beautifully written. I have not changed a single word, and this is what Harry Roberts said about Ronnie Kray:

I first knew of Ron and Reg Kray when I was 17. They were a few years older than me, so we were just acquaintances. As the years went by, I used to see them in the night clubs and restaurants around London.

I got to know Ronnie well when we were both locked up in the Special Security Block of Parkhurst Prison.

Ron was a really good guy. He treated everyone with respect and he expected to be treated with respect in return. Ron was always helping people. If he knew someone did not have the money for a visit from their family, he would make sure they got a visit or toys for the kids at Christmas. If he saw someone was short of a pair of weight-lifting boots, they would get a pair of weight-lifting boots. You could always rely on Ron to keep his word — if he said something was 'sorted', it was sorted.

Lenny McLean

Lenny McLean is, without doubt, the 'Guv'nor'. He is awesome. He's big, *massive*, standing at well over 6ft.

Lenny's a bare-knuckle fighter — the best, not only in this country, but in the States as well. He went to the USA and beat the Mafia bare-knuckle champion. He won $30,000 in one night. He was due to go back to his hotel room after the fight, but changed his mind and went directly to the airport as a precaution. Anything could have happened; gunmen waiting in the lobby or unwelcome visitors in the middle of the night, but Lenny was too cute for that. Nobody, including the Mafia, was going to take that $30,000 from him.

Lenny McLean's reputation preceded him, inevitably reaching Ronnie Kray in Broadmoor. Ronnie told me once that he had never met a tougher man than Lenny McLean. But that's not what really makes Lenny dangerous. Being tough is one thing; being tough and having a brain is another. Lenny is very intelligent — sharp as a tack. He's aware of everything going on around him, and even when he's talking, he studies every move, every look and every gesture. I suppose he has to in his profession — the business of violence. But he has used this quality in a constructive rather than a destructive way, having become an actor. He has been in films with Bruce Willis and has appeared in the TV programme *The Knock* and countless other shows.

Lots of people have had a pop at Lenny. He has

been stabbed on numerous occasions, and even shot, but he's very rarely been confronted face to face, because if you mess with Lenny, you are messing with the best.

I visited Lenny at his home on the outskirts of London to ask him if he was willing to contribute to this book. Lenny spoke very highly of Ron. He said:

Ronnie Kray was not brash or loud, although the media portrayed him that way. On the contrary, I found him quiet and humble, which surprised me. Ron's appearance was always very smart — his suits, his shoes, in fact, his whole presence, was overwhelming. The perfect gentleman. I was proud to be Ronnie Kray's friend.

And I know that Ronnie was proud to have known Lenny McLean, too.

Above: *(left to right)* Roy 'Pretty Boy' Shaw, Frankie Fraser and Alex Steen.

Below: Ronnie and Reggie enjoying a drink with some friends.

Above: Lenny McLean – 'The Guv'nor' – and I.
Below: Jeff Allen – one of The Twins' oldest friends – and I.

Above left: Charlie Walker.

Above right: Jack Lee.

Below: Billy Murray, who plays DS Don Beech in *The Bill*, and who was a friend of Ronnie.

(Left to right) Roy Shaw, Joey Pyle and Tony Lambrianou.

Above left: Ronnie and Reggie at home in Vallance Road.

Above right: Jimmy Nash.

Below: Ronnie and a friend enjoying a day out in the country.

Above: Ronnie *(left)* and Reggie *(right)* as youngsters.

Below: Ronnie *(left)* and Reggie *(right)* after their first professional fight at Mile End Arena.

Leo O'Reilly Jnr – a young boxer sponsored by Ronnie.

Top left: Albert Reading.

Top right: Ronnie Fields and I. Ronnie used to be my minder, and is a very close friend.

Below: A picture of me – one of Ronnie's favourites!

There are a few friends who warrant a mention who, for various reasons, I have been unable to contact. All have been, at one time or another, good friends to Ron. They are:

RICHIE ANDERSON
CHARLIE BRONSON
LES BURNHAM
JACK BINNS
TONY BURNS
FLANAGAN
JOHNNY FLEMMING
FREDDIE FOREMAN
FRANKIE FRASER
ANNE GLEW
FRANK HAYNES
JOHN GRIFFITHS
STEPH KING
RONNIE FIELDS
THE NASH BROTHERS
JOHNNY NEILSON
KEN STALLARD
ALEX STEENE
DOT WALSH
SHARON WOODS

If I have missed anyone out, I apologise.

7

Revenge is Sweet

Ronnie sent literally hundreds of letters to me during our relationship, touching on dozens of different topics in his spidery, sprawling handwriting.

But none shocked me more than the one in which he claimed to know that the former boxing champion Freddie Mills was murdered and who had killed him.

Freddie Mills was one of the most idolised fighters of his day. He was found dead in suspicious circumstances slumped in his car near his Soho nightclub. He had a bullet through his eye and a fairground rifle was lying close by. A Coroner's Court returned a verdict that Mills had killed himself, but no motive for such an act ever emerged and the mystery remains unsolved until now.

Freddie Mills was a pal of Ronnie's and he also listed dozens of showbusiness celebrities among his friends and was particularly close to gay 1960s singer Michael Holiday, who himself had committed suicide that same year.

Ronnie and I talked about Freddie Mills during my visits to Broadmoor. Freddie was a man Ronnie really admired, a real man's man and, because they were both boxers, they had shared a sort of special bond. I know of the rumours that had been flying about that Ronnie and Freddie Mills were lovers. On one of our visits I asked Ron if that story was true. Ron said that it wasn't. Friends yes, but no sex. He said that he respected the man, as a human being and as a great fighter and, anyway, he didn't like masculine types like Mills. He liked young, slim men in their early 20s.

Ron obviously knew a lot more about the whole business than he was prepared to say openly. Suddenly, right out of the blue, I received a letter from Ron. I thought it was bad news or that I had done something wrong. I had only seen him the day before and we had talked about my book. He was telling me stories to go in it. I thought we had covered everything.

Apprehensively, I opened the letter. The words screamed out at me: 'George Cornell killed Freddie Mills'.

I read it again. 'George Cornell killed Freddie Mills'. He wrote that Cornell had 'done him through the eye'.

I was shocked. It was fairly unusual for Ron to disclose anything like that, let alone write it in a letter. Ron had obviously told me a lot about his friendship with Freddie. They had been really good friends and, through Ron, I felt I knew him, even though I had never actually met him.

Life can be full of coincidences. At this point in my life I am heavily involved in the boxing world myself, which is unusual because it is very much a man's world. I have been asked to be the Press Officer for the newly formed UBO (United Boxing Organisation), which aims to co-exist with the British Boxing Board of Control. The UBO is an independent board which gives young fighters an opportunity to learn their trade in small hall fights.

Before I met Ron, I wasn't particularly interested in boxing, but Ron's enthusiasm and encouragement has rubbed off on me. When Ron was alive, he sponsored many young up-and-coming boxers, buying them their sports equipment on occasions. He encouraged street kids to put their time and energy into something productive like boxing. It kept them off the streets and out of prison. Many of them kept in contact with Ron, keeping him up to date on their careers, even sending him the odd trophy. Ron loved it and proudly showed off the photos of the young fighters to his visitors. One such boxer is a young man called Leo O'Reilly who started boxing at the age of 12. Ron saw an article about him in a local paper.

'He's going to go a long way, this kid,' he said to me, pointing at the cutting. Ron contacted the boy's family and offered to buy him his first pair of boots. Needless to say, the kid was over the moon. Since then, his success has accelerated. He never forgot that it was Ron who encouraged him. After every fight, he wrote to Ron to tell him the outcome.

Since Ron's death, the lad keeps in contact with me. On Ron's behalf, I keep up the sponsorship; I know Ron would have wanted that.

When I received the letter from Ron stating that Cornell had killed Freddie Mills, I already understood enough to know that what I was reading was explosive stuff. Here was this important information that Ron had kept a secret for years, and he wanted to share it with me. He must have thought long and hard before actually writing it down, but I had to laugh because there, written on the bottom of the same letter, was also his shopping list: six tins of sardines and twelve ounces of tobacco. I roared with laughter. Sometimes, Ron was so comical.

The next day, I went to visit Ron with the six tins of sardines and his tobacco.

'Did you get my letter?' he asked.

I told him that I had, but I didn't fully understand why he had written it. He said that he had told me about Mills so that I could put it in my book, the one I was writing at the time called *Murder, Madness and Marriage.*

Ron had written the letter on impulse. He had sent it on a whim but, typical Ron, he had had time to think about it, and inevitably changed his mind. Well, almost.

'Let me think about it for a few days,' he said.

He made me promise not to do anything with the letter until he told me it was OK. I wasn't too bothered either way. If he let me use the information in the letter, brilliant, but if he didn't, then I understood.

Ron took so long thinking about it, that I missed my deadline and I kept the letter in a safe place, under lock and key, until now.

On thinking about it, if Ron knew that George Cornell had killed Freddie Mills, what I didn't understand was why he hadn't said anything about this before. The evidence given at his own trial about why he killed George Cornell was that Cornell had called him a 'fat poof'. Ron told me that was all made up. It wasn't the real reason at all. In fact, there was more than one reason; first, killing Cornell earned him his 'button' (awarded when you've made a killing). And second, it enabled Ron to avenge the death of Freddie Mills, a man he admired enormously.

After Freddie Mills was killed, Ron vowed that Cornell would give his life for Freddie's. Ron knew that Cornell had killed Freddie Mills. If he had spoken up at his own trial, that would have cast a whole new light on the matter. It would certainly have provided a very strong motive for murder — Ron killing the man responsible for killing the friend he really admired.

Freddie Mills was killed on Saturday, 24 July 1965. He'd had a normal sort of day, quietly pottering about in his garden at his luxury home in Denmark Hill, South London, which he shared with his wife Chrissie and two daughters, Susan and Mandy. Later that evening, as usual, he went to his club, the Freddie Mills Nite Spot in Goslett Yard, Soho.

Freddie was a good host. He was the Peter Stringfellow of his day. Punters went to the club not only to see a World Champion Boxer, but to fraternise with the rich and famous. That night, Freddie was on good form and gave no indication of suicidal tendencies, as friends who were there at the time said later. On the contrary, that night champagne corks popped freely as he enjoyed what was to be his last evening alive. Nobody saw him leave the club in the early hours of that Sunday morning. He never returned home. Chrissie, his wife, was frantic with worry and went to look for him. She wished she hadn't.

She found him slumped in his car in Goslett Yard,

dead. He had been shot through the eye. Ron said that half of Freddie's brain was splattered on the back seat of his car.

It was a strange case. The coroner's verdict was that he had taken his own life, but the people who knew him best said that that didn't make any sense.

All kinds of stories started circulating — stories about Freddie's alleged homosexual affairs, his supposed money troubles. People said he'd been murdered. Of course, since Ron and Reg were London's leading gangsters at the time, some people also pointed the finger at them. And the finger has remained pointed in their direction for nearly 30 years. A few years ago, leading boxing journalist Tony Van den Bergh wrote in his book *Who Killed Freddie Mills?*:

> *One can only consider that the coroner's verdict was, from the police point of view, an extremely convenient one. They were already heavily involved with the most complex investigations into gang warfare in London and the possibility of a Mafia invasion.*
>
> *Further inquiries into this case might well have resulted in their having to expose more about their own operations than they would have wished. A verdict of suicide might well have been one they were ready to accept, in spite of the questions it left unanswered. And, by the time Nipper Read reopened the case, years had passed and the trail was cold.*
>
> *If Mills, then, didn't pull the trigger, who did?*
>
> *There is no sound evidence against either the Krays or the other leading gang at the time, run by the Richardsons. The Krays had become*

*convenient scapegoats who could safely be blamed
for any unsolved crimes ...*

Ron, of course, had always been well aware of the
stories that had done the rounds; the story that he
pulled the trigger, and even the story that he was
involved in a homosexual affair with Freddie.

Ron told me that he didn't have a sexual affair
with Freddie and I believe him. But Ron did say that
Freddie was bisexual and he also said that he did
have an affair with Michael Holiday. Freddie
wanted to have an affair with Ron, but he was not
Ron's type. Ron said Freddie liked powerful men,
he got a kick out of the 'power trip'. The more
powerful, the better. Maybe this was the reason that
Cornell killed him. This begs the question: was it
George Cornell in Goslett Yard with Freddie Mills
that fateful night?

When Ron told me on the visit not to publish the
letter that he had sent me, not for a while at least, I
didn't mind. I knew the letter was of great
importance, but the timing had to be right before the
truth was told. A couple of days later, Ron phoned
me and told me to sit on the letter. He had decided,
for whatever reason, that the time was not right.

The next time I saw him, he said that I was to put
the letter in a safe place. I was to show no one and,
more specifically, tell no one.

Ron never said any more about the Mills
business. I honestly don't know whether it can be
true or not. I know it's stretching coincidence to it's
limit but, on the other hand, I never knew Ron to lie
deliberately — unless, of course, he was in court!
Perhaps he was trying to blacken George Cornell's
name. But Cornell was a scum bag and everyone
knew that, and Ron never needed to justify killing

him. Perhaps Ron really did know the answer to the Freddie Mills mystery.

I think Freddie Mills' death was the nail in the coffin that finally persuaded Ron to kill George Cornell. But, of course, Ron was also determined to get his 'button'. He instantly selected Cornell as his target in the underworld ritual known as 'getting your button', resulting in being a 'made man'.

I had heard the expression before I met Ron, but I couldn't remember where. When Ron told me that he was a 'made man', I was puzzled.

He explained that the four major gangland bosses from the four areas of London formed a pact, just like the Mafia Godfathers, that they would all look after each other's interests.

There would be no poaching of their rivals' territories, and to seal this bond each gang boss would carry out a very public killing as a token of their commitment to this treaty.

Ron said the execution of Cornell was his bloody signature to the pact.

I laughed. I thought he was winding me up.

'Stop pulling my leg,' I said.

Ron looked deadly serious. 'I'm not,' he replied.

I know this all reads like gangland fiction, but I came to know how real it all was when I saw the names of the pallbearers on the service sheet at Ron's funeral and the message that went with it from Charlie and Reg.

We wish for only good to come from Ron's passing away and what is about to follow is our tribute to Ron. It is a symbol of peace in that the four pallbearers will be Charlie Kray, Freddie Forman, Johnny Nash and Teddy Dennis, each one represents an area of London, North, South, East and West.

They all encircled Ron's coffin and stood for a minute's silence.

I believed Ron when he told me he 'got his button'. It was no joke; the look on his face told me that.

Whenever Ron spoke about George Cornell, his face distorted with hatred. He said that Cornell was a bully and that was one of the things he hated most. Ron said that Cornell was also a big-mouth. He was loud and brash. Ron couldn't stand him. When Ron found out that he had killed his friend, Freddie Mills, he was livid.

'Cornell was bragging in a pub that he shot Freddie,' Ron seethed.

Ron stubbed his fag out in the ashtray and immediately lit another one. He was getting wound up.

'Don't get wound up, Ron,' I said.

Too late.

'You don't understand. He put the rifle against his eye. Before he pulled the trigger, he tried to make Freddie squirm.'

Ron lit yet another fag and continued. 'Freddie told him to "get fucked". Freddie Mills was a brave man. He wasn't scared of anyone. He was a World Champion boxer for fuck's sake. Cornell was a mug. He wasn't fit to walk in Freddie's shoes.'

I interrupted Ron. 'How do you know he tried to make him squirm?'

'Because he was fucking bragging about it in The Blind Beggar. The slag. He thought if he killed Freddie he would be a 'made man'. When Freddie told him to 'get fucked', he stuck the rifle in his eye and blew his brains out.'

Ron was mad. I tried to interrupt again but he continued talking over me.

'When I heard that he blew Freddie's brains out, I swore, one day, I would blow his fucking brains out and I always do what I say.'

On 9 March 1966, Ron kept that deadly vow. Ron heard that Cornell was drinking in The Blind Beggar on Whitechapel Road in East London. Ronnie told Reggie that it was about time he dealt with Cornell.

'I'm going to do the bastard tonight,' he said.

Ron washed and shaved, went to his wardrobe and chose one of his many suits which were hanging in a neat row.

Carefully, he put a 9mm Mauser hand-gun in the right-hand pocket of his cashmere overcoat. He looked in the mirror and nodded his head. He felt good.

'I'll pass with a push and a pull,' he muttered.

He swaggered down the stairs and motioned to his driver.

'Let's do it.'

His driver snatched the car keys from the kitchen table and drove Ron to The Blind Beggar. It was early evening; the roads were empty. His car pulled up outside the pub. Ron got out. He shrugged his shoulders, straightened his tie and coolly walked into the pub. Cornell was sitting in the near-empty bar with two of his side-kicks. He smirked, 'Well, look who's just walked in.'

Ron never said a word. He walked towards the bar, took the gun out of his pocket, aimed at Cornell's head and fired. He was dead before he hit the carpet.

Cornell's drinking buddies dived for the floor, as did the two or three terrified customers who had been sitting nursing their pints. The barmaid screamed. The record on the jukebox jammed and started to blast out, again and again, the line of the song it had been playing: 'The sun ain't gonna shine any more, the sun ain't gonna shine any more ...'

Ron strolled out of the pub. He was on a high. He later told me that at that moment, the moment he shot Cornell in the head, he felt fucking marvellous.

Ron said that Cornell glared at him as he pulled the trigger. Ron laughed.

'His brains made a good pattern on the wall. I smelt fear on him and I loved it,' he said.

When Ronnie got back to the pub where Reggie was waiting, Ron told him what he had done. Immediately, they made their way to another pub. They went round the side entrance as they did not want to be seen. They banged on the door.

The landlord opened it to find Ronnie and Reggie standing there, Ronnie covered in blood. Nodding at his brother, Reggie said, 'He's just killed George Cornell.'

The landlord was scared but let them in and showed Ronnie to the bathroom. Ron took his clothes off, climbed into the bath and scrubbed himself in a bid to wash away the blood and brains. Not easy. It was nasty, sticky stuff, coating him from his hair down. Hardest of all to remove were the powder marks which had scorched Ron's hand.

He changed into fresh clothes brought from their aunt's house in Vallance Road. He washed his jewellery and watch and burnt his paper money. Ron's bloodstained clothes were stuffed into a suitcase, then taken away to be burned.

Another friend, Charlie Clark, the burglar known as the Cat Man, disposed of the gun, the gun that evaded the police despite extensive searches, the gun which came into my possession so many years later.

Ronnie waited anxiously for news of the killing, passing the time with friends having a few drinks and a cheese sandwich. He turned on the *Nine O'clock News* to hear that there had been a fatal shooting in the East End. He took another bite of his cheese sandwich, looked at his brother and smiled.

Later that evening, Ron was back home, fast asleep. The police hammered at his door and took him into custody for questioning. He declared his innocence. The police arranged for an immediate identity parade. Eye-witnesses, who had been in The Blind Beggar, could not — or would not — pick him out of the line up. Much to Ron's delight, he was released.

The police could prove nothing. No one was talking. But they knew — as everyone who knew anything about anything in the East End knew — that Ronnie Kray had killed George Cornell.

Now Ron had really lived up to his nickname of the 'Colonel', given to him by the Firm because of the precise way in which he organised 'business' and because he loved a battle; the bloodier the better.

*　　　　*　　　　*

1967 was the year of the beginning of the end for Ronnie. It was also the year of what has since been described as his greatest coup: the springing of a villain called Frank Mitchell, known as the 'Mad Axeman', from Dartmoor prison.

The strange disappearance of 'Mad Axeman' Frank is one of the legendary stories of London's gangland in the 1960s. He was one of the Kray firm's toughest heavies. An enforcer so big and so vicious no one contradicted anything he said. If on a Tuesday Frank Mitchell said it was Thursday, then it was Thursday. No one dared argue with the big nasty bastard, but he loved the twins and was a key player in their criminal empire and was prepared to do almost anything Ron and Reg commanded. Inevitably, he ended up inside as a Category 'A' hard-case prisoner, a man feared by just about every screw who ever dealt with him.

But Ron needed him out for a major job he had got planned. In a brazen operation which typified the ever-increasing power of the Kray gang, the twins organised Mitchell's escape from Dartmoor, then Britain's harshest prison, in 1967.

The escape was planned with military precision. Reggie even did a recce and made a trip to Dartmoor. He contacted a friend, former World Boxing Champion Ted 'Kid' Lewis, and asked him to write to the prison Governor offering to give a talk to the cons about his boxing career and show some films of his fights. Ted mentioned that he would be accompanied by three friends. Of course, Ted had no idea why his friends wanted to visit Dartmoor.

Unbeknown to the authorities, one of them was Reggie who, just for fun, also brought along two of his friends, ex-cons with long list of convictions.

An enjoyable day out was had by all — especially as the Governor treated Ted and his group to a splendid meal after the show and urged them all to 'call again'. With a straight face, Reggie assured him they'd be delighted.

Shortly afterwards, Frank Mitchell was with an outside working party when he quietly slipped away from the other prisoners. At a pre-arranged point, he met two members of the Firm, who bundled him into a car. He was back in London before he had even been missed.

He was never seen again and, to this day, his disappearance remains one of the great gangland mysteries which surrounded the Krays. The twins and members of their firm were arrested and stood trial at the Old Bailey. All were acquitted.

No one really knew why this great brute of a man should be sprung from prison only to be killed and his body disposed of with such clinical efficiency that not a single trace was ever found.

The story Ron told me reveals a simple, but basic, motive for the removal of Frank 'Mad Axeman' Mitchell.

Ron said that once Mitchell was sprung from the nick he was put up in a nice comfortable flat over a shop in Plumstead, in south-east London, and told to keep his head down for a few weeks until all the fuss had blown over.

When Ronnie went down to Plumstead to see him after a couple of days, he asked Mitchell if everything was all right and if there was anything in particular he wanted. Mitchell looked at him and said, 'Ron, after five years inside there's only one thing I want at the moment, and that's some crumpet.'

It was natural enough, I suppose, and Ron agreed that he would find a nice-looking prostitute who would do the business with Mitchell, at Ron's expense of course.

But Ron was worried that things were still too hot and that a prostitute might tip-off the police about Mitchell's hide-out.

He said he needed to find a brass who would not grass and Ron thought there might be a problem with the girls being frightened of going with Mitchell because of his reputation for being a complete animal.

Rumours had it that Mitchell was kinky. He was into bestiality, meaning copulation between a person and an animal. He instigated this act with women whom he forced against their will to perform sexual acts with dogs. He constantly read pornographic material feeding his depraved obsession.

Mitchell got more and more restless as each day went by and kept asking Ron when they were going to bring the woman.

After six days, Mitchell could wait no longer. He was really steamed up and threatened to go out and look for a tart himself. Ron warned him not to step outside or it would blow the whole operation. At the same time, he was being fed on the best steaks and any other grub he wanted. Boy, did he know his way to the pantry. He ate like there was no tomorrow. He was getting fitter and stronger by the day. But the only thing Mitchell hankered after was a woman. Finally, he couldn't, or wouldn't, wait any longer. He waited for Ron to arrive at the flat. Nervously, he paced the floor muttering.

He heard a car pull up outside the flat and peered through the net curtain. It was Ron. He hardly had time to get through the door when Mitchell blurted out, 'Where's this fucking tart you promised me?'

Ron tried to pacify him, explaining that it was a bit tricky to fix anything up at that moment and he'd just have to hang on a bit longer.

Mitchell was having no excuses. Suddenly, Mitchell turned on Ronnie, grabbed him by the lapels and threw him against the wall, yelling at him, 'Look, if you don't have a woman for me in this flat by tomorrow, I'm going round to your house and I'm going to fuck your mother.'

Ron's eyes narrowed. That sealed Frank Mitchell's fate. He had committed the cardinal sin — he'd insulted Ron's mum and nobody did that. He had also laid hands on Ronnie and nobody did that either.

So Mitchell had to die in a way suitable for such a beast. Under normal circumstances, Ron would never of been in the company of such a man. Ron always maintained that a person's sexual preference was their own business, but having sex with an animal was stretching the realms of decency too far. Still, Ron overlooked this disgusting behaviour because he needed Mitchell for business, but when Mitchell trashed his mother he had overstepped the mark.

Ron wasted no time. Later that same evening, he gave the word and three shifty looking men arrived at the flat where Mitchell was staying. They told Mitchell that it was getting too hot at the small flat above the shop in Plumstead. He was being moved to a safe house in the country. There, he could have as many tarts as he wanted.

Mitchell sat on the sofa in the lounge smoking a fag and reading one of his porno magazines. Two of the men sat at the kitchen table playing cards.

Another stood by the window keeping watch making sure the coast was clear, from time to time peeking through the net curtain. Under the cover of darkness, Mitchell was led to the waiting van. The engine was running. The driver lit his roll-up for the umpteenth time.

Mitchell bent his huge torso almost in half as he climbed into the grey Commer van. The three 'faces' climbed in behind him. Once inside, the van was locked.

Ron told me later that the man who killed him said, 'Mitchell was a bugger to kill. He sat in the back of the van. At first he was chatty. Then it suddenly dawned on him. He realised it was all coming on top. He knew his life was in danger but it was too late.'

His assassin took the gun from his inside pocket and pulled back the trigger. Mitchell looked him in the eye. Nobody spoke.

BANG. The first bullet thumped into his body. He slumped forward on to his knees clutching his heaving chest. Blood oozed from the gaping wound. He gasped. His executor stood astride his helpless victim.

BANG. BANG. BANG. He emptied the clip into the lifeless body.

Ron's eyes shone as he told me that story. It was obvious he was telling me the truth. He had no reason to lie. He was already serving life so if he had killed Frank Mitchell then he would have told me. I asked Ron what had happened to Mitchell's body. He laughed. 'He was fed to the porkers,' he replied.

Ron was still angry. He found it difficult to tell me what Mitchell had said about his mother. He scowled.

'He was a no-good bastard and deserved to die in the worst possible way. He should never have said what he did about my mother. It took me a while to think of a fitting end for him. Then I remembered an old friend who owned a pig farm in West Kingsdown, Kent.'

I saw real hatred in Ron's eyes. He was reluctant to tell me any more but I insisted.

He said that Mitchell had been a big old lump and weighed about 20 stone. It took a few 'faces' to carry his lifeless body to the farm at West

Kingsdown on the Kent and London borders. There it was chopped up and fed to the pigs, a fitting end for a man who enjoyed watching sex with animals.

I don't think for one moment that Ron was winding me up. Others have a different tale to tell. I have heard lots of different stories of the whereabouts of the big fellow.

One story had Mitchell's body taken out to sea, trussed in chicken-wire with concrete weights attached, and thrown overboard.

There was also a rumour that it was buried under a motorway bridge, along with the body of Ginger Marks, another casual acquaintance of Ron's who also disappeared mysteriously in the late 1960s.

It was another of those macabre legends in the life of Ronnie Kray.

*   *   *

Ronnie talked about death and punishment as easily as most people talk about the weather. It was a way of life — his way of life. Over the years he developed deep and dangerous fixations about three men. He told me that if he ever got his liberty, those three men would die.

Top of Ronnie's Hit List was the former Scotland Yard detective who smashed the Kray empire. He was known to all, good guys and bad guys alike, as 'Nipper' Read.

This dogged police officer now lives in contented retirement but he's rolled out occasionally for his quotes on all matters relating to the Krays. He had a deep hatred of Ron. Ron felt similarly about Read. Ronnie had an obsessive hatred for 'Nipper'. He organised a massive gang-busting raid on the East End on 8 May 1968 — and he led from the front.

Detective Superintendent 'Nipper' Read and a squad of armed officers arrived at 43 Braithwaite House, Bunhill Road. The long-awaited moment for Read had arrived. With their .45 calibre Webley pistols drawn, they proceeded to kick down the door of the sleeping Kray twins' flat, whereupon Ronnie and Reggie were arrested and taken into custody. Everybody thinks that Reg and Ron were charged and convicted with one murder apiece. That's not true. 'Nipper' Read had spent many a long hour compiling a Charge Sheet as long as your arm.

Ron and John 'Scotch' Ian Barrie were charged with the murder of George Cornell in The Blind Beggar public house.

Ron, Reg, brothers Chris and Tony Lambrianou, Ronnie Bender and Anthony Barry were charged with the murder of Jack 'The Hat' McVitie.

Ron, Reg, Tommy Cowley and Richard Morgan were charged that, on the days between 1 January and 6 May 1968, they had conspired together with other people, to murder a Maltese known as 'George Caruana'.

The prosecution alleged that a member of the Firm had hired Paul Elvey, a 'pop-pirate engineer' to kill Caruana. Elvey, said the prosecution, would have used either a powerful crossbow or an explosive substance under a car to murder Caruana, who had 'homed in' on their enterprises.

Ron, Reg and Tommy Cowley were charged that, on various days in 1967, they had conspired together and with other persons to murder a man. The prosecution claimed that this time they plotted to use Elvey to kill a man whilst he was actually in the Old Bailey. According to the prosecution, Elvey planned to use an attaché case, in which was fitted a poison-filled hypodermic syringe which could be operated when the case was swung against the body of the victim.

Ron was charged with causing grievous bodily harm to a man in 'Esmerelda's Barn'. The prosecution said that because the man was supposed to have annoyed him, Ron invited him to the club, paid his taxi fare, and then placed a red-hot poker against his cheeks and shoulders.

Reg, Ron and Charlie were charged that, in 1964, they had demanded from Leslie Payne and Frederick Gore the sum of £5,000 with intent to steal it.

Reg, Ron and Charlie and several others were charged that they had conspired to defraud people by pretending that certain bonds, stolen from banks and penthouses in America and Canada, were theirs, and could be negotiated either for loans or for sale.

Finally, the Krays and eight others were charged that they had conspired together to cheat and defraud those who might be induced to supply goods on credit to a series of companies in which they had an interest, including: S Crowther and Co; Lanni Caterers Limited; Six-Two-Five Centre Ltd; Carston Securities Ltd; Dominion Refrigeration Ltd; Anglo–American Traction Finance Ltd; and Overseas Development Ltd.

After all this was added the charge that the Kray brothers, Whitehead and Donaghue murdered Frank 'Mad Axeman' Mitchell. Another charge was that those five, along with Connelly, Cowley, Garlick and Dickson conspired between 1 November and 23 December 1966 to effect the escape of Mitchell from Dartmoor prison and then received, harboured, comforted and assisted Mitchell, with intent to prevent, hinder or interfere with his being taken into lawful custody.

'Nipper' Read had been busy. He had waited a long time and gathered as much evidence as he possibly could against Reg and Ron. He knew he had only one chance and he was not going to waste it.

He wanted his pound of flesh and he wanted to see Ron get what he thought he deserved. He was there at the start of the arrest when Ronnie was pulled out of his bed and taken into custody and he was there when he was eventually sentenced to life.

Ronnie told me that he would never forget the look on Read's face when he was sentenced. He said he was smiling and shaking everyone's hand as if he'd won the bloody pools. From that moment on, Ron developed an obsessive hatred of 'Nipper' Read and conspired on several occasions to find a way of taking revenge on the man who had put him behind bars. 'Nipper' Read was, hardly surprisingly, top of Ronnie's hit list.

Another name to feature high on the list was that of Mickey Duff, the boxing promoter. The origins of his loathing are obscure. But both men had their roots in the fight game where passions invariably run high and punishments are enacted with force inside and outside the ring.

Ron never told me why, but he had a loathing of Duff and used to call him 'that bastard Mickey Duff'. One day, I asked Ron why Duff was on his hate list. On this particular day, Ron was in no mood for small talk. His eyes narrowed and he scowled.

'He's a slag. I sent him a dead rat through the post. He deserved it. I should have killed him when I had the chance.'

Ron stubbed his fag out in the ashtray and lit another one. He always did that when he got the needle. I thought I had better not to pursue the matter of the dead rat in the post and 'Ol' Duff's' involvement.

Another to feature as a candidate for death was a two-bob crook called Peter Gillette. He had the audacity to visit Ronnie wearing dirty trainers and jeans. He is now serving a long jail sentence for his part in a major drugs racket.

Ron really hated Gillette. He saw him as a jumped-up little nobody clinging on to the tails of the Krays to try to bring himself a bit of kudos. Gillette thought that he was Reggie's number one. He used to tell everybody that he was Reggie's adopted son. He was 33 years old for Christ's sake! Ron would cringe with embarrassment whenever he read it in the newspaper.

But Gillette thought that by saying he was Reggie's adopted son, it gave him an edge over everyone else; it made him special. The mug. So when it was announced that Ron and I were getting married, I think he saw me as a threat. To what, I've no idea. But in his tiny mind he decided to try and spoil our wedding plans. Reggie didn't come to our wedding all because of one man — Peter Gillette. For that, Ronnie never forgave Gillette.

Even now, I find it hard to write his name. To me, he will always be Slag Gillette. Or just Slag for short.

Reggie thought he was a good friend. In mine and Ronnie's eyes, he was mistaken.

It's not a very pleasant story, but probably the most ironic part of it is that it was Ron and Reg who saved his life. If it wasn't for them, Gillette could have been found floating face down in a river somewhere a long time ago.

I knew Gillette because I'd occasionally delivered some papers to him from Reggie. That wasn't unusual — I delivered lots of things to lots of people.

I was friendly with Gillette but no more than that. To be honest, from the start, I thought he was a prat. Later, a woman detective was quoted in the newspapers as saying that he was so obsessed about his looks that 'if he were a chocolate he'd eat himself!'

When we met it was 'Hello, how are you?' A peck on the cheek maybe, perhaps a quick chat, but only out of politeness. Nothing more. As Ron said, 'Good manners cost nothing.'

So when we read in the paper that he had said I'd had sex with him, I was horrified. So was Ron. I read the newspaper, burst into tears and couldn't stop crying. The phone rang and it was Broadmoor — Ron couldn't ring himself at that time. They said, 'Ron's really upset and wants to know if you're all right. Ron says you must come up and see him.'

I said 'No'. It wasn't that I didn't want to see Ron. He was the one person I did want to see, but not all those other people. All I wanted to do was run away.

Broadmoor rang back. 'Ron's really insistent,' they said. 'You've got to come.' So I went. I looked terrible; big puffy eyes, big fat nose and my face all red. I waited outside until everyone went in so it looked like I was late. Ron was waiting for me.

I felt as though everybody was looking at me. But as soon as I walked into the visiting hall, Ron stood up. He put his arms around me and made a big fuss of me. I'll never forget how Ron did that. He was showing everyone that he knew the story was rubbish and that he was supporting me.

Ron was brilliant. I started to cry, but Ron would have none of it. He didn't want me crying in front of all those people. And, anyway, what did I have to cry about? I'd done nothing wrong. He knew that. He told me not to worry, he'd sort it.

He tried to cheer me up but he was upset, too. I could tell. Most of all, he was angry. I'd never seen him so angry.

Over the next few days, there was a lot of activity around Ron. He wanted to see his most trusted friends. I was present on some of the visits and not on others. Ron was mad — really mad. He wanted Gillette sorted.

'Kill the bastard,' he ordered one of his friends.

A few days passed. Reg tried to smooth things over with Ron. There were more comings and goings. Ron would not let it go.

'Hurt him. Hurt him bad,' he whispered to a close friend.

It was there I heard him tell his friend to hurt Gillette.

A few weeks later, the same man was back on a visit.

'It's sorted Ron,' he said.

Ron smiled. He wanted him dead, but he settled for him being hurt. I heard through the grapevine that he was shot in the leg but Gillette does not realise how close he came to being fed to the porkers.

There was certainly no shortage of offers to do the job, but Ron said he wanted to finish it himself when he got out.

With Ronnie, you thought sometimes that his hates and talk of revenge were just fantasy. But then you would hear that someone had been 'done' in one of the prisons, and Ronnie would have that sort of twinkle in his eyes and would give one of his sinister laughs.

Then perhaps I would have to take a payment to

someone to pass on to the person who had 'done' the prison job. I knew Ronnie still had the power and the influence to make things happen.

Peter Sutcliffe, the Yorkshire Ripper, is living proof of that. It only took a week for Ron's decree that Sutcliffe should 'be marked for life' to be carried out. And Sutcliffe was in Parkhurst on the Isle of Wight at the time.

When Ron heard what had happened to Sutcliffe, he was sitting in his cell in Broadmoor watching the television news. He smiled and gazed out of the window at the beautiful Berkshire countryside. He lit another cigarette ... another job well done ... time to plan the next one.

So I knew from experience that Ron was not all talk. I knew that anyone on his death list would have remained in danger until the day Ronnie died.

His favourite phrase for talking about someone with whom he had fallen out was 'he's been ex'd'. He referred to his brother Charlie several times as 'Charlie ex'. It happened the first time after Charlie had visited him and failed to bring him even a packet of cigarettes. I fell out with Ron several times myself and was told that I had been ex'd. He once wrote to me as 'Dear Kate X'. But it never lasted long; a few days later he would be back to normal and would say, 'Come on, me old dutch, forget all about it. I can't help myself sometimes; it must be the German in me.'

With someone as unpredictable as Ronnie, you never knew when you might suddenly find yourself on his 'Ex Files'. Just like a Mafia Godfather, he never forgot.

Ron was obsessed with the Mafia and his great ambition in life was to rule a crime syndicate to match the feared Sicilian organisation which reached almost every corner of the world.

Those who knew him have little doubt that he would have succeeded had he stayed at liberty to fulfil his dreams. Like the Mafia bosses he idolised, Ronnie had a clinical ruthlessness when disposing of his rivals and a shrewd mind for business, both of the criminal and legitimate kind. This was partially curtailed by his occupancy of a Broadmoor cell, but far from extinguished completely.

In fact, Ronnie ran a flourishing organisation along Mafia lines, with its tentacles reaching throughout Britain, inside and outside jails, financing big-time crime, and ordering or arranging punishments. He drew protection money on a vast scale, taking 'retainers' from other criminal gangs so that they could use the Kray name in their criminal enterprises.

In Ron's heyday, it seemed easy and no one could stop the Kray twins. They went from strength to strength. It seemed that the twins were untouchable.

Everyone, including the American Mafia, wanted to do business with them and, as a result, Ron flew to New York to meet the Mafia bosses. It was the beginning of a friendship — and business arrangement — that lasted until Ron's death. After that first meeting, Ronnie and Reggie were soon repaying their hospitality in London. Ron met with a representative of the American Mafia, a businessman from New York, to talk about setting up an international operation, with Ron representing the Mob interests in the UK. It offered all concerned the potential to accumulate untold power and wealth. The plan never came to fruition, but that didn't stop Ronnie from playing a chilling Godfather role until the day he died.

In Broadmoor, Ronnie would meet criminals

from all parts of this country as well. Whenever anyone was coming to see him, he would really look the part. He would wear one of his many hand-made suits, starched shirt, silk tie and crocodile shoes, and hold audience just like a Mafia baron.

In return, his visitors were always expected to dress up smartly as well to show their respect. Ronnie hated anyone coming to see him sloppily dressed.

I was on a visit with Ronnie one morning when he said he had a business meeting with a man who was coming all the way from Liverpool. He was expected at 10.00am. He must have left Liverpool at the crack of dawn to get to Crowthorne for that time of the morning, bearing in mind he must have been pre-warned not to be late for the Colonel's visit.

On the dot of ten he was shown into the visiting hall. I looked at him. The screw pointed to where Ron and I were sitting.

'I think this is your business associate Ron,' I said laughingly.

Ron scowled. He put his drink down and extinguished his cigarette. I could not believe the man who was walking towards us.

He looked like a train-spotter. He was wearing a blue-and-red nylon anorak. And would you 'Adam and Eve' it — he had the bloody hood up!

Ron stood up. The man put down his Tesco carrier bag and held his hand out to shake Ron's.

'You must be Ronnie Kray,' he said in a Scouse drawl.

Ronnie furrowed his brow. I saw him take a deep breath. I looked away, trying not to giggle. I picked up my teacup and buried my face whilst attempting to drink the lukewarm tea. I knew Ron was going to say something, and it was not going to be pleasant.

He motioned with his hand as if he was shooing ducks away, flicking them with disgust. As Queen Victoria once put it, he was not amused.

He could barely speak he was so cross. He sucked his lips against his teeth. His eyes narrowed. His speech was shaky with anger.

'How dare you ... How dare you come to see me dressed in such a way? Go away. Just go away.'

The train-spotter was dumbfounded.

'But ... but, Mr Kray ...'

Ron turned his head in disgust and, with one final gesture, the train-spotter was dismissed. There was no arguing or pleading with Ron. In fact, there was no room for negotiation.

Ron sat back down at the table and watched the train-spotter disappear out of the visiting hall, dejected and demoralised.

I turned to Ron with tears of laughter in my eyes and put my hand up to my mouth and said sarcastically, 'You was a bit harsh, weren't you?'

Ron didn't think it was funny. 'It's a fucking liberty, that's what it is,' he snapped.

That's what it was like with Ron; catch him at a bad time and you were sorry.

*   *   *

However unpredictable he was with male visitors, Ron was always so polite and charming in the company of women. He would always stand up whenever his female visitors entered or left the room.

I remember the first time I met Ron. I was bowled over by him.

I arrived at Broadmoor early. It was a cold September morning in 1987, grey and frosty.

I was nervous. I must have changed my outfit a

dozen times. I put on a black suit. No — too morbid. I put on a red short skirt. No — too tarty. I settled for a classy silver-grey French number. It was at the time when big shoulders were in fashion making my waist look narrow for the first time. I looked in the mirror and smiled. I'd pass with a push and a pull.

The M25 had been a bloody nightmare, more like a car park than a motorway. I wanted to make a good impression and arrive on time for my first visit with Ron. Reggie, who had become a friend, had warned me that Ron hated anyone being late for his visits.

I left at 7.00am to get to Crowthorne in Berkshire for 10.00am. Needless to say, I was far too early. I made my way to the old Victorian side of the asylum. It looked so bleak. It reminded me of the old black-and-white film *Oliver*, that scene from the workhouse of long cold corridors, khaki-green-painted brickwork, and big heavy iron doors, shut and bolted. Every fibre in my body wanted me to turn on my heels and run. Visiting Reggie in prison was one thing, but going into Broadmoor was quite another. I suppose in a way, deep in my subconscious, I believed what I had read in the newspapers — that Ronnie was mad.

I didn't know what to expect. Maybe he would have his jumper on inside-out or his glasses upside-down. Perhaps I was nervous of Broadmoor and not Ronnie. I really don't know. I wanted to go home but I had given my word that I would visit.

I walked into the reception area. It was like walking into another world. It felt cold. I shivered. It is hard to describe the pungent smell of confinement that only a Victorian asylum has. A mixture of sensations including despair, fear and madness. It must take years for it to develop.

At the end of the room, standing behind a glass screen, stood a burly, no-nonsense-looking man. Nervously, I approached him.

'I've come to visit Ronnie Kray,' I said in a hushed tone.

Realising it was my first time at Broadmoor, he smiled.

'Sign the Visitor's Book,' he said as he turned a huge book towards me that was resting on a swivel pivot. It was massive. My eyes scanned the powder-blue pages.

First question: Name? That was easy — Kate Howard. Address? Simple.

Reason for visit? I panicked. My mind was racing. What if I put the wrong thing? Oh shit! What was I doing here? How could I answer it when I didn't know myself? Actually, I was there to pass on messages from Reggie. But I couldn't put that. I know. Play it safe. Social visit.

Next question. Relationship with patient? What was I? There he was, Ronnie Kray, famous gangster, and I was going to see him. What could I say, when I had never even met him? I know. Friend.

Again, I looked at the officer. He motioned with his head.

'Take a seat.'

I sat back in the plastic seat and sighed. I looked at my watch. Forty-five minutes to go.

The first thing that strikes you when you go to Broadmoor is the unreal atmosphere of calm in the place. It's a spooky feeling but strangely enough, peaceful. No one spoke as we walked along the corridors and through the sets of doors until we arrived at a room which looked like a school assembly hall with a raised platform and lots of Formica-topped tables and chairs.

The nurses head-counted us into the hall. I learnt afterwards that they always do, as they will never allow the visitors and the patients to move about at the same time. The patients are moved in one at a time and you have to wait until they are seated at a table before you can join them. Or vice versa; you sit down first and the patients are escorted to you. You can't both arrive or leave at the same time. Necessary, I suppose, for security.

I looked around the hall at the men sitting at their tables, trying all the time not to look nervous. There was Ron. His eyes were transfixed on me. If I hadn't known he was gay, I would have sworn he fancied me. I knew it was him, of course, because he looked just like Reggie. I couldn't believe my eyes; he looked every bit the gangster.

He was wearing a beautifully cut, navy-blue pin-striped suit. A crisp white shirt with double cuffs and, on his finger, a gold pinkie ring.

As I walked towards him he stood up, gave me a kiss on the cheek and, holding the chair out for me, said, 'Come and sit down next to me. I've heard a lot about you from Reggie.'

I could not get over how softly spoken he was, how polite and how gentle. This was not the man the newspapers had portrayed at all. He smiled. I melted.

I told him I'd brought some letters and some food and had put them in the special box at the main gate. He nodded, thanked me and asked for any news. I told him I had spoken to Reg. He was looking at me carefully. Ron always sat right up close to you and he never raised his voice. I just kept looking at him and listening to him intently. The other patients and their visitors were just feet away, but I didn't see anyone else in the hall. Ron had this thing about him. It's hard to describe. A kind of aura. You didn't want to look anywhere else. He had soft brown eyes and they held you.

Everyone says the same thing about meeting Ron. They didn't expect him to be so gentle, so they're surprised. They were drawn to him. He had charisma, that's the word.

'Got any news?' he asked again.

So I told him all the news and we chatted about everything and anything. I couldn't get over how nice he was.

He ordered me tea.

'Allow me,' he said as he started to pour the tea. 'I must apologise for not having any decent cups and saucers.'

He held my arm and said, 'You look lovely.'

I was speechless.

'Your suit. It's smashing.'

He went on to compliment me on my skin, my hair, my teeth. I should have been flattered that he said so many nice things, but coming from a man who had been incarcerated for over 20 years and having only had the company of men, I thought he probably would have complimented a stray dog.

Even so, I was flattered. I was sure he meant it and he proved his sincerity by asking me to marry him on my second visit. And, eventually, I said 'yes', which surprised many people — including me. But Ron had real charisma. It was only the harsh side of Ron that was ever portrayed, only the character of the ruthless gangster. That was one side of him, the side that men saw if they crossed him. The other side, the side he displayed in the company of women, was a softer, kinder side, a side of Ron men never saw. He knew how to treat a lady and women loved it and loved him no matter what their age.

Even old ladies in the visiting hall were won over with chocolates and fluffy toys.

He did it just to see them smile. Some became emotional probably because they had never received a gift from a man in their lives unless it had a plug on the end of it! Ron was not like that.

He just wanted to treat all women the way he treated his mother, with courtesy and respect. It was the sort of old-fashioned manners people didn't expect from a Kray. But murderers can have manners, you know.

8

Mrs Kray

'This is Kate. Kate Kray. Wife of ... Ron Kray.'
This is how I'm introduced. I am never
introduced as just Kate. If I'm honest,
sometimes I don't mind. It depends whose company
I'm in. At times, it's embarrassing, at other times it's
useful.

One of those useful times, when being a Kray
was to my advantage, was when I was driving along
and the police pulled me in for a routine traffic
check. The officer looked at my driving licence and
read my name. Without looking up, he laughed.

'No relation to Reg and Ron I suppose?'

'Yeah, I'm Ron's wife ...'

He was fascinated and out came the usual
barrage of questions. He quickly forgot why he had
stopped me — a good result, as I had four bald tyres
and no tax or insurance at the time!

On the other hand, I have experienced many
embarrassing situations. For instance, the time when
I applied for a mortgage. I sat in a small office

waiting to see the building society manager and in he walked with an official-looking folder under his arm.

'Sorry to keep you waiting, I must apologise,' he said as he sat down at his official-looking desk. He got out a huge number of forms and began to fill them in. He started asking me official-sounding questions. Things were going smoothly throughout the interview. Every now and then he would pipe up with, 'Can't see any problem with your application ...'

But then we got to the part on the application form where they require details of spouse,

'Name?' he said, without looking up.

I thought I might just as well leave now, but I considered bluffing it. No, I thought, give him a try. So I answered him.

'Ronnie. Ronnie Kray.'

He stopped writing and bit the end of his biro; still he didn't look up. I could almost hear the alarms bells sounding in his brain.

'Mmm ...' he pondered. 'Ronnie Kray as in Ronnie Kray?' he tentively enquired.

Now our eyes met. I nodded.

'That's the one.'

Nervously, he dropped his biro on the official-looking papers.

'Will you excuse me a moment, Mrs Kray?'

From that moment on, I knew I did not have a chance in hell of that mortgage and I hadn't even got to the question of Ronnie's occupation! So you see, being a Kray has its advantages and disadvantages.

*   *   *

I first became involved with 'the Kray Twins' early

in 1987. I was 32 years old and my 13-year marriage to Harry Howard was over. I was drifting, unsure where to go or what to do next. I'd heard of the Krays, of course — who hadn't — but I'd never really given them much thought. Why should I?

One day, I was wandering around the book shop on Charing Cross station. I had been on a shopping trip to London and was fed up because I had missed my train.

I was killing time until the next train arrived, when I saw a book about the Krays called *The Profession of Violence* by John Pearson. It had David Bailey's famous photo of Reg and Ron on the cover. It was the first time I had seen a picture of them.

On the spur of the moment, I bought it. Something compelled me to buy the book. I was intrigued and curious, and I did something I'd never done before — I wrote a letter to someone I'd never met, Reggie Kray. It was only a jokey letter and I never in my wildest dreams expected a reply, so I was chuffed when I got a letter on my birthday.

We wrote to each other for a while, then right out of the blue he phoned me.

'Hello, it's Reggie Kray here ...'

I was speechless! Reg asked me to visit him. I suppose, initially, I was curious. He sent me a visitor's order and I made the long journey to Gartree prison in Leicester.

Security at Gartree is tight. I was nervous. All the other visitors went into a big hall, but an officer came up to me and said, 'Mr Kray has asked to see you in the private room at the end of the hall.'

I sensed the other visitors watching me and

nudging each other. The officer showed me into a tiny room with just one table and two chairs. I came in one door and Reggie came in another. We sat down and there were all these screws watching us from outside the door. Before I had a chance to speak, Reggie motioned to the door and yelled, 'Shut that door.'

I started to laugh. 'You sound just like Everard!' I said, and he did, just like Larry Grayson in the TV programme. He burst out laughing. Well, at least it broke the ice. After that, we hit it off straight away. The visit went brilliantly. But before it had ended he said that he had never met anyone with my sense of humour before ... and I must meet Ron.

I think I now understand, as well as anyone can, the relationship between Ron and Reg, but it was all a bit of a mystery in those early days. Every time Reg wrote to me and every time I saw him, he'd ask me to visit Ron. Reggie and I had become good friends, but throughout that friendship his main concern was for Ron. He never stopped asking me to visit him. To be honest, I was a bit scared of meeting Ron. With all the things I'd heard about him, I thought he was probably a raving lunatic. Then there was the place — Broadmoor, a hospital for the criminally insane. Just those words were enough to scare the pants off me.

I didn't want to go to see this man or the place, but Reggie was my friend and very insistent so, in the end, after a year of nagging, very reluctantly I agreed to go.

It was at the time of the postal strike at the end of 1987 that I eventually made arrangements to go to Broadmoor. Reggie wanted some letters delivered to Ron. He asked me to take them and I was left with no alternative but to go. At that first meeting with Ron, I didn't realise that my life was about to change for ever. Straight away, Ron and I struck up a special kind of bond. Reg must have known instinctively that I was the right person for Ron, and that our sense of humour was the same. Maybe he felt, and rightly so, that I could lighten things for him and make him laugh again.

Reg made me laugh one day when he wrote to me saying that he was glad Ron and I had decided to marry, He wrote, 'Ron is a good-looking chap.'

I roared with laughter; what a thing to say — they are identical twins!

After a year of Ron asking me to marry him, we eventually tied the knot in Broadmoor Hospital on Monday, 6 November 1989. Our wedding was bizarre to say the least. Ron left all the arrangements to me.

Typical man! I wanted to make our wedding special. It was important to me that things were right.

From the day I said 'Yes', Ron didn't want to know the whys and wherefores. For three weeks I was like a complete nutter, as I had to arrange two wedding receptions. One inside Broadmoor and one outside.

I had to see the Catering Manager at Broadmoor to talk about our buffet, wedding cake and flowers. There was my dress to have made, the car to arrange and the guest list — Oh, God, that bloody guest list! It was a frantic time. Apart from doing all the organising, I was visiting Ron every other day. If he changed the guest list once he changed it a hundred times.

'Put this one on, he's gotta come; take him off, he's a slag, he can't come ...' It drove me nuts. It's a wonder that I wasn't kept in Broadmoor. Ron wrote to most of the guests, I phoned others. By the time we'd finished the list for the 'outside' reception, it had 200 names on it.

Broadmoor allowed us to use the Tribunal Room for our 'inside' reception. It's a room where the patients are told if they have been granted parole or not. The room itself is plain, and looks like a headmaster's study. On one wall stands a trophy cabinet filled with tarnished trophies. The small window on the other side of the room was heavily barred with curtains which dated back to the 1960s and were a disgusting bright orange with brown triangles. It was the best Broadmoor had to offer, so it had to do.

The Catering Manager was brilliant.

'You can have what you want,' he said, 'so long as you pay for it.'

It sounded good to me. Money wasn't a problem.

'Right, for a start, I want the nicotine-stained ceiling covered with pink-and-white helium-filled balloons all with trailing ribbons falling from the ceiling. I want the florist to come in and fill the place with fresh flowers.

I want the food table covered with crisp white linen with garlands of fresh flowers and greenery.

For the centre-piece on the table, I want carved ice dolphins. The food I want fresh lobster, caviar and more seafood. Oh, and turkey for people who don't like fish and Caesar salads.'

I want ... I want ... I want ... my mother would have slapped me.

Next, I contacted the Hilton Hotel in Berkshire. There, I had to go through it all again. This time for 200 guests.

Our big day arrived. It was a freezing

November evening. The ceremony was scheduled for 5.00pm. The eight guests whom Ron eventually chose to attend the ceremony included Joey Pyle — Mr Big, the newspapers called him. He's been a good friend of Ron's for a long time. Not so long ago he was branded Britain's number-one criminal for smuggling drugs worth half-a-million pounds.

I don't know about all that, but I've always liked Joey. He was there the first time I met Ron at Broadmoor and he's been a good friend to me ever since. I've always thought he looks a bit like Terry Venables. In fact, when I was with a friend in a restaurant once, and the waiter told us a man wanted to send us over a drink, I thought it was Joey. It wasn't — it *was* Terry Venables!

Next, there was Alex Steene, a London boxing promoter and entrepreneur. Alex was a real dude and looked more like a gangster than the gangsters! Unfortunately, Alex died of a massive heart-attack whilst I was writing this book. He was the Peter Pan of the underworld — forever young. He always wore a long, white mac over his suit and a pair of shades. He wore those dark glasses whatever the weather, day or night, all the time — weddings included!

Then there was Johnny Nash, one of the Nash brothers, who are both businessmen from East London. Ron wanted to invite him. I had never met him before. He struck me as a very quiet man and I liked him when I met him at the wedding, although I haven't seen him from that day to this.

Another guest was Paul Lake, a very talented young artist who had painted Eric Clapton and was doing a picture of the twins at the time. He's a good-looking man and really nice, too, but I don't think his painting of Ron and Reg was one of his greatest successes. Before Ron saw the painting everyone was telling him what a brilliant likeness it was, and how young he looked. Ron was a very modest man and said to them all, 'I'll wait until I see Kate. She'll tell me the truth.'

And I did. It was the most horrible painting I've ever seen. Reggie looks like a Toby jug and Ron looks like he's just bitten someone's head off!

Ron asked me on the next visit. 'What did you think of the painting, Kate?'

I looked at him and giggled. 'It's OK to put above the fireplace to keep the children away from the fire.'

Ron screamed with laughter and said, 'I knew you would tell me the truth.'

Then there was the twins' brother, Charlie, of course. There were two other men whose names I can't remember, who were doing a bit of business with Ron at the time and, finally, Ron's Best Man, another patient at Broadmoor, Charlie Smith. He's in his late 30s now but he's been away since he was 17.

Charlie was high on drugs when he stabbed a man to death in a park. Once he came down and realised what he had done, he gave himself up to the police and, of course, was imprisoned. But Charlie wasn't well. He went completely mad and strangled his cellmate, so they put him in Broadmoor.

All our wedding guests had to be checked out by the Home Office, although I'm not entirely sure why. I shouldn't think the IRA could get anyone out of Broadmoor and you'd have to be some kind of magician to smuggle anything in.

But there was one other guest Ron wanted to invite whom the Home Office turned down flat. It was Charlie Richardson, the London gangster Ron had known for donkey's years. I don't know why they wouldn't let Charlie come, it seemed a bit unfair.

I suppose some people might be surprised that Ron wanted Charlie at our wedding at all. After all, the Kray and the Richardson gangs had been at each other's throats back in the old days, sometimes literally. And, of course, George Cornell, whom Ron shot, was a member of the Richardson gang.

But that was all a very long time ago and Ron and Charlie ended up as good friends. Charlie visited him in Broadmoor once and Ron gave Charlie a beautiful 1950s' solid silver cigarette case.

The other guest — probably the most important one — who was supposed to come but didn't, was Reggie.

Ron and Reg had had a row just before the wedding, and Reg said he wasn't going to come. So Ron said, 'Don't bloody come, then.'

Then Reg said he would, and then he said he wouldn't, and then he said he would. In the end, the nick said, 'Sod it, too much mucking about, you're not going,' and that was that.

But Ron always thought that Reggie would change his mind and come for his sake. He was wrong. The first words Ron said to me on our wedding day were 'Have you heard from Reggie?' His face dropped when I said I hadn't.

We all assembled in the small Tribunal room. The Catering Manager had done what I had asked. The ceiling was covered with pink and white helium-filled balloons. Big mistake. For the whole of the service, the ribbons continually aggravated the sullen gangsters. I overheard one of them remark, 'Them fucking balloons are doin' my 'ead in.'

I wore a peach-and-cream silk taffeta dress especially designed by Aneska. It was a boned basque top with a double skirt.

I thought I looked gorgeous but, with hindsight, I looked more like a bloody meringue. Nobody knew what to say.

The registrar asked me if I took this man as my wedded husband. I replied, 'I do-Ron-Ron, I do!'

Well, at least it broke the ice. Ron looked at me and shook his head. Until then, the room had been dead quiet. But now, all eight men were grinning.

'Nice one, Ron!' one of his friends called. Ron laughed. There were loads of screws standing around the room, more than two for each guest. What were they expecting — a riot? But they had probably never seen such a group before — at least a group who were going to be allowed out in an hour or so! It was really quiet. The men didn't like it with all those screws there. It was terrible, really.

Then the Registrar asked Ron and me for details.

'Father's occupation?'

'Carpenter,' I said.

Ron thought for a moment. 'Wardrobe dealer,' he said.

I looked at him. Wardrobe dealer? I mouthed silently, and started laughing.

'Well, it's true,' he whispered, and it was. Years ago, that's what they used to call men who went totting from house to house.

Next question. 'Occupation?'

'Proprietress of a chauffeur Rolls Royce service,' I wrote.

The Registrar looked at Ron and smiled and, with the devil in his eyes, Ron smiled back.

'Er ... I think we'll leave that blank, Mr Kray.'

We signed the Marriage Certificate and that was that. I was officially Mrs Kate Kray ... wife of ...

From that day on, my life was turned upside-down.

Being married to Ron was never dull. Each day was different. I enjoyed his company immensely. Our sense of humour was the same and although there was a 23-year age gap, it never bothered us. It bothered lots of other people, but not us.

In the few years we had together, we had more fun and laughter than most married couples have in a lifetime. Our marriage was a loving one although never consummated. Therefore, our relationship was based on friendship. Unlike any 'normal' married couple, the time we shared together was spent talking, a rare commodity in most marriages.

We never got bogged down with the normal arguments of every day living, like 'What's for dinner?' or 'Where's my clean shirt?' I never had to nag him to mow the lawn. And I knew where he was every night.

We had our occasional ups and downs but nothing major, so when Ron said he was going to divorce me, it hit me hard and I never fully understood why. To this day, I don't know the real reason. I can hazard a guess though.

One thing I know for sure is that Ron did not want a divorce. We were getting along OK, just fine. We always did. We would laugh and joke all the time. I would try to lighten things, defuse situations. Ron liked that.

Like the time when a dwarf sold his story to a Sunday newspaper. He claimed that he was a hit-man for both Reg and Ron. I happened to be visiting Ron on that Sunday morning which was unusual as he preferred mid-week visits when the visiting hall was not as busy. When I arrived on the visit Ron was hopping mad.

'Have you seen the paper today?' he growled.

Before I had time to answer, he snapped, 'It's a liberty. That's what it is. He was never a hit-man for me.'

I tried to contain my giggling.

'What's so funny?' he snapped.

'What's so funny? A dwarf claiming to be a hit man. Are you sure? Think about it, Ron. Was kneecapping his speciality?'

Ron roared with laughter. He saw the funny side of it then. I made a joke out of an otherwise explosive situation. The dwarf doesn't realise how lucky he was. A gun-toting dwarf. What next? That's the relationship Ron and I had. It was a pretty good one, too. It worked for us.

But then Ron became ill. One day I'd visited him and he was fine, the next visit he was a totally different person. Things went from bad to worse almost overnight. It was obvious that he wasn't right, I could tell by his eyes. As soon as I had sat down he made me take off my glasses. He snapped, 'You're not Kate. Who are you?'

I took my glasses off and tried to pacify him. But it was no good. Try as I might I just couldn't reach him. He was sick. The worst I had ever seen him.

I left the visit that day feeling pretty miserable. I decided that I would leave him alone for a while. That usually did the trick. If I'm honest, though, I had a gut feeling that this time things were different. I had never seen Ron so paranoid.

My worst fears came true a few days later. Early one morning, my phone rang. It was

Broadmoor. Straight away I knew it was trouble. It was Carol Barnes, Ron's social worker. She said that there had been an incident and that Ron had attacked another patient, a man called Lee Kiernender, a big bloke in his early 30s. I asked her if it was bad and was Ron all right. She said that Ron was OK but the other patient had been throttled half to death.

As a result, Ron was being moved on to the intensive care ward. It's called the intensive care ward because that's exactly what happens. It offers one-to-one care for inmates when they are in the depths of their madness.

I drove to Broadmoor immediately as I wanted to see Ron. His doctor explained how very ill he was and that he thought it would be better for Ron and myself if I didn't visit him for a while, at least until they got him stable again. I agreed to stay away for a few days, thinking that that would be better all round.

A week later, Ron phoned me. His speech sounded slower. It was barely audible. He wanted to see me. I was glad. I thought that he must be getting better and that the rest had done him some good. With hindsight, I should not have gone. He just wasn't ready for visitors. I had guessed by his voice that his medication had been increased but I hadn't reckoned on how much. It wasn't often that I refused Ron anything. So when he insisted that I go to see him, I agreed. I wish I hadn't.

The man I went to see wasn't the Ron I knew. He was not the gentle, mild-mannered person I had fallen in love with. I could not talk to him and he did not want to listen to anything I had to say. We had a terrible visit, resulting in me telling him that I would never go and visit him again whilst he was on the intensive care ward.

I know that sounds harsh given the state of Ron's mind, but with a strong man like Ron I had to maintain his respect. If I had let him walk all over me, I would have lost that respect for ever. Our relationship would then be over.

I left the visit that day in tears. I was hurt and angry. I didn't feel that I deserved being treated in such a harsh way. Tears streamed down my face as I drove my car down the M25 on my long journey back home.

I muttered to myself that no way was I ever going to forgive him. I meant it. No matter what.

But I couldn't stop caring about him overnight. I just couldn't turn my affections off like a tap. If only life was that simple.

So I continued to phone him every night at 8.00pm. I didn't know if the staff told him I still rang, or if he still waited for my call. It didn't matter. I felt compelled to ring, just to see if he was OK.

I never heard anything for a few weeks. The divorce papers arrived, out of the blue, on the morning of Friday, 22 January 1994. Ron had started divorce proceedings. Strangely enough, I laughed. I wasn't too bothered. I felt that Ron was making a point. A stand. But I figured that given a day or two he would change his mind.

He was like that about everything. If he asked me or one of his friends to do something, we would always wait a few days before we carried out his orders in case he changed his mind. Ron changed his mind almost daily. So, at this point, I didn't take the threat of divorce seriously.

I know that he would definitely have changed his mind if only people had left him alone. It seemed like the world and his wife kept interfering. People around Ron were always vying for position, trying to win favour with him, but I was his wife. He trusted me. I had never let him down.

I was there through thick and thin. I saw the mugs come and go. Ron discarded them like yesterday's newspapers.

At first, I used to fight the mugs. I don't mean physically, nothing like that. I mean I was constantly proving myself to them and Ron. Mind you, one of these mugs, who was doing business with Ron at the time, phoned me one day and told me he was going to kill me. I laughed and called him a fat bastard and said he couldn't kill anyone. When I told Ron what I had said, he it found amusing.

'That's it, you tell him, you're a Kray now,' he said.

Although he made a joke of the incident, I later found out that he had given the man a 'tug' for talking to me in such a manner. Needless to say, Ron didn't do business with him any longer and I never arranged any more visits for him.

That's the way it was around Ron — everyone jostling for the number-one position so they could later lean on the bar in the pub bragging.

'Course, you know me and Ronnie Kray are like that ...' as they held out their crossed fingers. The cocky bastards.

In the end, I got to the stage where I didn't want to fight any more, I felt that I had proved myself enough. I was tired. I didn't need it.

Then I received another letter from Ron's solicitor, stating the reason why he was divorcing me. He was divorcing me on the grounds of unreasonable behaviour! I couldn't believe it!

In the series of events around this time my book *Murder, Madness and Marriage* was published. It couldn't have been published at a worse time.

When I was writing the book, Ron had been fine. He was keen for me to write it and was happy to help me with a lot of the stories in it. It was a joint venture and we split the money between us. Later, when it was serialised in the paper, Ron was furious about one story. No, nothing to do with his violent past. He was livid that I had said that Ron wanted the same Hollywood teeth as his brother Charlie. Charlie had visited Ron and showed off his brand-new capped teeth. Afterwards, Ron said, 'Kate, I want you to get me something.'

'What?' I said. 'New vests?'

Ron shook his head.

'Cigarettes? Sardines?'

'I want teeth like Charlie's,' he said nonchalantly.

'WHAT!' I threw my hands up in disbelief and shrugged. 'You want teeth like Charlie, then you shall have teeth like Charlie.'

I fixed up for a dentist to go in, and soon he had a mouthful of gleaming white teeth!

I was being flippant, and if Ron had been in his normal frame of mind he would have probably found it amusing. But being ill, he was furious to see the story in cold print.

Later, the papers claimed that Ron was divorcing me because I had revealed in the article that I had a boyfriend. That's not true. Ron knew all about my boyfriend. Indeed, if Ron had not given me permission to have a boyfriend then, believe me, I wouldn't have had one. Well, not one who'd remain alive, anyway.

Ron was a sensible man and realised I needed someone and, as long as I didn't mug him off by taking him to any of the gangster dos, or drag him around where any of his friends were, he didn't mind a bit. In fact, it was his idea. The strain of being married to Ron was beginning to show. I felt I had lost my identity.

I wasn't just Kate any more; I was Kate Kray ... wife of ... I didn't mind but, at times, I needed to be just Kate and talk about me, my thoughts, my feelings. Ron sensed this.

'What you need, my girl, is a boyfriend,' he said, wagging his finger at me.

'Yeah, I know, but who's going to take me on?'

Ron laughed. 'That's your problem,' he said. 'None of my friends will go near you out of respect for me and people who don't know me won't go near you out of fear of me.'

He definitely had a point, but nothing is impossible.

So Ron was not upset about the boyfriend. He wasn't really upset about the book. He was just upset in general.

Our now crumbling relationship was at a delicate stage. I didn't think it could possibly get any worse. It just goes to show how wrong one can be.

To my horror, Ron had a suspected heart-attack. Broadmoor phoned me and said that Ron had been taken to a hospital on the outside. I raced up the motorway to see him immediately. I arrived at Harewood Hospital to find it under siege. Photographers and reporters were everywhere. I knew I had to dodge them as I was in no mood to talk. I went through the maternity ward in order to avoid their prying cameras.

The grounds of the hospital were littered with marksmen and plain-clothed officers on guard. They were ready for ... I just don't know. Ron had had a suspected heart-attack, for Christ's sake.

I made my way to the ward where I knew Ron

was being kept. Huge plain-clothed officers stood guard like ferocious Rottweilers. I approached them and introduced myself. 'I'm Kate Kray ... wife of ...'

They looked at each other. I saw the suspicion in their eyes. 'ID, please,' they snapped.

I gave them my passport as identification. Every one of them insisted on looking at it.

Eventually, I was allowed into the main ward. Ron was in a private room at the end of the corridor where another five or six officers were sitting. Again, all of them wanted to see some ID before they allowed me in. I heard Ron before I saw him.

'I want a fag,' he yelled. 'Give me a fag.'

I laughed. I knew he had been giving them a bit of hassle. I opened the door and poked my head round. Ron was sitting up in bed wearing striped pyjamas, opened, to allow the electrodes to be attached to his chest.

I remember it well as it was the first time I had seen my husband in pyjamas and in bed. He had a hospital tray in front of him and was eating his dinner. He stopped eating and looked at me. He didn't have to say a word.

I could tell he had the hump. I was hoping he was feeling better, but I was wrong.

'This is all your fault,' he growled. 'Do you realise I have had a heart-attack? I could die.'

I felt terrible. The screws sitting at the end of the bed looked at me. Ron was relentless. He wanted someone to blame. I wanted to do something to help. I offered to go to see the doctor to find out what was wrong with him.

To be honest, I wanted to get out of the room, it was very claustrophobic. We didn't have any privacy; the screws could hear every word Ron was saying to me.

It took ages before I spoke to a doctor and when I asked if Ron had suffered a heart-attack, his reply was 'No'. In fact, Ron at that time had a very low potassium level and was advised to eat lots of bananas. All that fuss, and all he needed to do was eat bananas.

I walked back into the room where Ron was waiting for news.

'Give it to me straight — I can take it,' he said.

I looked at him and shook my head. 'You ain't had a heart-attack. You are low on potassium. The doctor said you've got to eat lots of bananas.'

Ron's face softened. A big, broad grin spread across his face.

'You fucking actor,' I said. 'You ain't goin' to win no Oscars.'

The screws started to laugh and so did Ron. I was happy. We were back on an even keel and Ron gave me a kiss and told me to forget everything he had said because he didn't mean it.

I left the hospital satisfied knowing that Ron was OK and, more importantly, we were friends again.

But it wasn't to last. In a day or two he had changed his mind again; the divorce was back on. To be honest, I was exhausted by it all.

I was living in the real world where bills have to be paid. I had to work. I had to earn a living. I couldn't concentrate with Ron's roller-coaster of emotions and madness I had let things slide long enough.

He continued to write to me. He didn't say much, he was too ill; I knew because his handwriting was a scrawl. It was hard to read at the best of times, but now, even I had trouble reading his letters. The gist of them was that, as soon as he was better, he would make things up to me.

I wanted to believe it so I always signed my replies: 'From your X-wife Kate — ha ha.' Always the joker. A bouquet arrived with a simple note from him: 'To my wife Kate, love Ron.'

That said it all, but in the next post more divorce papers arrived. I didn't reply to a single one and I never signed any of them. I knew Ron did not want a divorce. I couldn't understand why it was still going ahead.

Eventually, though, the decree nisi divorce papers arrived stating that we were divorced. I was shocked to think that he had allowed it to go that far. Deep in my heart, I always hoped he would change his mind. I honestly believed he would, but he was not very well and never had the strength to stop it. Maybe he just gave up, not only on us, but on himself.

Six weeks later, the final divorce papers came through. Ron phoned me; he seemed better. I asked him if he was OK and what the matter was. He sounded sad. He asked if we could still be friends. I told him that we would always be friends, but he wanted me to visit him. I was torn. Part of me wanted to see him and part of me didn't. I loved Ron but not his illness.

For me, the divorce made it final. I didn't see any point in it any more, although I didn't say that to him. I told him I needed a bit of time to recover, to gather my thoughts. Although my heart was telling me one thing, my mind was telling me another. He had divorced me, it was in black-and-white that we were no longer man and wife.

But I knew in my heart of hearts Ron didn't want that and neither did I. Once the divorce had started, it was like a runaway train, we were powerless to stop it.

I expected Ron to sort it, to stop it, but he didn't. Maybe this was the one thing that was beyond his control. I wanted time to digest the series of events. Ron understood. He even said sorry, and tried to laugh the divorce off and asked me to forgive him. I told him God would forgive him, but could he forgive himself? I would have forgiven him in time, but I never realised that time was the one thing we didn't have.

Although I had refused to visit him, it didn't stop him ringing me. He rang me often. Every night, almost. I didn't mind; I was glad that Ron and I were friends again.

Then, suddenly, on 17 March 1995, Ron died and, on 5 July 1995, so did my father, making 1995 the worst year of my entire life. Many factors contributed to this, apart from Ron's and my father's deaths. It also coincided with me being made bankrupt. My life was at a crossroads. I didn't know what to do or where to go. I thought that I needed a clean break. First, I found a new place to live. It was smashing. I moved in with my boyfriend. It was a new beginning, or so I thought.

My new-found happiness lasted just two weeks. 'Rat' as I refer to him now, who had moved in with me, started to 'play up' because he wanted to attend Ron's funeral. That was out of the question. He didn't know Ron, so why the hell should he go? I would not allow it. I didn't care what he said, the answer was 'No'. He got the needle. I was shocked.

I thought it was me that he cared about. I was wrong — it was Kate ... wife of Ronnie Kray. It was the old kudos thing again. We had a terrible row and he left.

I struggled to pay the high rent on my flat. It was the first time that I had lived on my own. I hated it. When I was married to Ron, I wasn't on my own because my sister Maggie moved in with me.

After a while, 'Rat' began to telephone me and say how much he missed me and how much he loved me. He begged me to let him come home. At this point he was seeing someone else, although I didn't know it. He phoned me every day, pleading with me to let him come home.

It was Wednesday, 5 July 1995. The phone rang. I looked at the clock. It was 7.30pm. I knew it would be 'Rat' because I hadn't heard from him all day. I had decided that the next time he phoned, foolishly, I was going to agree to give him another chance. I suppose I had missed him. We stayed chatting on the phone for an hour-and-a-half. I told him he could come home in the morning but he didn't want to wait that long. He wanted to come home straight away. I weakened. He said he would be there in half-an-hour. I hung up smiling.

Almost immediately after I had replaced the telephone, it rang again. It was my sister; she was screaming. At first, I thought it was screams of laughter. She was uncontrollable.

'He's dead! He's dead!' she yelled.

My blood ran cold. My skin seemed to tighten. In my heart, I knew what she was about to say but I didn't want to hear.

'Daddy. It's Daddy, he's dead.'

I dropped the receiver. Not my Daddy. Not my Daddy. He can't be. I couldn't breathe. I tried to take a breath but I couldn't. I wanted ... I wanted ... my Daddy.

'Rat' arrived. He and my other problems seemed to fade into insignificance. He took me to the hospital so I could see my dad. It was the worst night of my entire life.

Earlier that evening, he had pleaded with me to let him come home. I said he could. Now, when I needed him most, he decided he had changed his mind. He said that he couldn't cope.

He couldn't cope! The dirty bastard took me home the night my father died and he left me. I was alone.

Arrangements were made for my dad's burial. He was Irish and wanted to be buried in Ireland. We had two services, one in England and one in Ireland. 'Rat' came with me to both. He didn't accompany me because he wanted to comfort me. I should be so lucky. The only reason he came was to stop anyone else from putting their arms around me to comfort me. He was insanely jealous and he always had been. Not only with me but any other girlfriends he had.

'Rat' and I made the long trip to Ireland. We flew there because 'Rat' said that he was tied up with business and could only stay for one night.

My mum paid for those tickets. Everyone else in my family travelled by ferry from Fishguard to Rosslaire.

We flew into Dublin where my Uncle Ned picked us up from the airport. 'Rat' stood guard making sure that nobody kissed me or even put a comforting arm around my shoulder. Dad's funeral was beautiful. I was in shock, grief stricken. 'Rat' said that he had to fly back immediately. We didn't even have time to go to my father's wake. We caught the next available flight home. He dropped me off and disappeared. I was alone again.

Already devastated by Ron's death, I had the death of my dad to contend with. My entire family was still in Ireland. I had no one to talk to, no one to turn to, no shoulder to cry on. Thinking back now, I don't know how I coped.

I phoned 'Rat's' sister. She was sympathetic.

'Don't shed any tears over him,' she said. 'He ain't worth it. He's got another bird.'

I could not believe it. All the time he had been messing me around, he had another girlfriend. He put me through absolute hell with his pathetic jealous rages. He had accused me of having an affair with the world and his dog, and all the time it was him being unfaithful. The filthy bastard.

His sister said that if I wanted to catch him redhanded, then all I had to do was go to his birthday party which was planned for the end of July. I never knew anything about his birthday party.

By 10.00pm on the evening of the party, I knew I had to go, just to see for myself, once and for all, if the rumours were true.

His sister and I had gone out earlier that evening for a drink. I couldn't enjoy myself; all I could think about was that party. So I returned home and changed my clothes from a pretty dress to black jeans and a black jumper, suitable attire for surveillance. I carried a CS gas canister with me and drove to Gravesend in Kent.

The party was in full swing at the address I had been given. I looked for 'Rat's' car amongst all the others parked around the house. Loud music was blaring from the garden. I didn't see his car so maybe he wasn't there. I decided to walk around the back and have a look over the fence.

The fence was high so I had to keep jumping up and down trying to see, but I was too short and my legs ached. So I made a little hole in the fence by moving two slats, and peered through it.

I saw an Arab sheik walking around, and then I saw Robin Hood and Batman. I was confused. Only then did I realise it was a fancy-dress party. But I didn't see 'Rat'.

Then I spotted him. He was dressed as General Custer. He wore a hat at a jaunty angle. He had his arm around a cow-girl. I watched through the hole in the fence as he kissed her.

The dirty bastard. His sister was right. I wondered what I should do. Should I leave and confront him later? But that would leave it open for him to deny it. Or should I walk into the party and confront him there and then. He would not be able to deny a thing. Fuck it. I went into the party.

The guests were mostly travellers and the cow-girl seemed to be a traveller herself. I could tell because she was wearing the obligatory large, gold hooped earrings, despite her costume. Yee-haa.

The chances are that if anyone walked into a party held by travellers and started a row, then it was quite possible they would get hurt. I didn't think about it. I was too angry to care. The mood I was in, I would have killed anyone who got in my way.

That night I felt like a commando on manoeuvres. I pulled out my gas canister and slipped into the party unnoticed. I stood by the swimming pool and just watched. My hand squeezed the gas canister.

Someone was singing on the Karaoke machine. It was Robin Hood.

'Crazy ... I'm crazy for feeling so blue ...'

Suddenly, General Custer spotted me. His face turned to stone. He mouthed the words, 'Hello, darling, what are you doing here?'

What happened next seemed to be in slow motion. Slowly his arm fell off the cow-girl's shoulder. I started to walk towards him. Other guests noticed me and got out of the way.

Robin Hood was still singing, 'Cray ... zeee ... I'm crazy for feeling so blue ...'

As I walked towards him, he was trying to act as if he was happy to see me. His mind must have been going ten to the dozen trying to work out what he was going to say.

He needn't have bothered. I was far too angry to listen to anything he had to say.

The only way he could have stopped me was if he had had a gun. He would have had to shoot me dead to stop me from gassing him in the eyes. He screamed. Right beside him was a small picnic table with bottles and glasses on it. I picked up a bottle and hit him over the head with it. The bottle smashed and it cut him over his eye, blood poured down his face. He was screaming in agony like a stuffed pig.

Still Robin Hood didn't stop singing, 'Crazy ... I'm crazy for feeling so lonely ...'

'Rat' tried to get me out of the party. I careered into him. His American soldier's hat fell off. He felt around on the ground for it and put it back on his head. Every time he put that fucking hat back on his head, he put in on square then adjusted it to an angle.

I can only assume on reflection that, when he was fitted with the General Custer costume, the assistant must have told him that General Custer did not wear his hat square on his head, he wore it at an angle. Jauntily. 'Rat' must have had that on his mind. I'd gassed him and bashed him but still that hat remained on his head, come what may. Jauntily.

Eventually, we got out of the party. By now, he had regained some of his sight, but tears and blood were streaming down his face. He was blubbering, 'You've got it all wrong. I love you.'

He must have thought I was a right mug. I punched him in the mouth. He copped one for Ron dying and he copped one for my dad dying; in fact, he copped one from every angle. I was the maddest I have ever been. Boy, did I lose my temper.

No one person came out of the party to stop the row. 'Rat' looked for something to hit me with. He was half-blinded from the gas.

Suddenly he remembered his sword hanging on his belt. He drew it. It wasn't just any sword, it was a General's sword with a gold fucking tassel on the end.

He started to wave it about as if he was a brave soldier in a bloody war. But his sword was plastic and it wobbled. He waved it about in the air. It sounded like Rolf Harris's wobble board. He brought it down hard across my cheek.

I didn't feel a thing. I shrugged off his plastic onslaught.

'Well, that fucking hurt, didn't it?' I sneered.

At this point, I noticed a shiny gold earring which he had never had before. He must have thought he looked pretty cool. I ripped the earring out of his ear, pinged it in the gutter and poked him hard in the chest.

'That's it. You've made your last stand, Custer.'

I walked away. He followed me, screaming and crying for me to go back.

'Please don't go,' he sobbed.

I turned and looked at him. He grabbed my arm. I retaliated and knocked his hat off again. He picked his hat up and put it back on his head — at an angle.

He got mad and picked up a house brick and threw it at my car, breaking my back window. Then another. He was hurling them at me. I started to drive away and he grabbed hold of the door handle. His hat came off again, so I reversed over it and flattened it.

My last image of 'Rat' was in my rear-view mirror picking up his now flattened hat, punching it out in defiance and putting it back on his head — jauntily.

It was General Custer's last fucking stand.

That was the end of 'Rat'. The end of 1995.

I was on my own again.

*　　　*　　　*

As the well-known phrase states, the grass is always greener on the other side. Lots of women have told me that they would give their right arm to be in my position; to have no children, no ties, to be able to please themselves, to do what they want, whenever they want, and not to have to consider anyone else. No shopping in Asda every Friday, rushing home to do someone's dinner, washing, ironing, cleaning, asking if it is OK if they ... blah ... blah ... blah.

Well, I don't have to do any of those things. I can do exactly as I please. Take, for instance, last week. A good friend of mine called Ashleigh phoned me and asked if I wanted to go to America with her for a month.

'It won't cost you a penny,' she said. 'Pack a bag and we will just go.'

I thought for a bit, trying desperately to think of a good excuse why I couldn't go. But, in reality, there was no excuse. I just plain and simply didn't want to. A lot of people would have jumped at the chance to have a free holiday in the States. A holiday of a lifetime.

But not me. It's not what I want. It really isn't. In fact, I long for normality. A normal home. A normal lifestyle. A normal man.

Someone asked me, if I had a choice, what I would like most in the world. I had no hesitation — to be with a man who loved me. But what I would really like most, but cannot have, is a family.

When I was married to my second husband, Harry, we tried for 13 years to have a baby. We tried just about every treatment under the sun, none of which worked. Eventually, I became very ill. I collapsed at home. I had a tumour in my womb and it burst, poisoning my blood stream. I nearly died. I was admitted to hospital, which resulted in me having a hysterectomy. I was totally devastated. At first, I wanted to die.

Most women long for a baby, and there are still times when I could just throw myself off a bridge, the yearning is so great.

Whenever I see a baby, every time I hold a little one, it's there, that yearning. It never goes away.

And people can be so insensitive.

'Oh, I wish I was like you,' women say to me. It's all right for them, they have usually got two or three lovely kids.

'All that time to yourself, that freedom. If I had my time over again ...'

But it's crap. They don't mean it, and I feel like getting them by the throat and yelling, 'Don't fucking patronise me.' The pain inside cuts like a knife. Sure, it eases with time, but it's a dull ache that never really goes away.

I have been able to cope with it better in the last few years by being lucky enough to get to know Dolly, the daughter of a very dear friend. Dolly is 16 and a beautiful young girl. From the moment my friend introduced us, we clicked. She calls me 'Mum'. She always has. She sent me a Mother's Day card. It was the first Mother's Day card I have ever received. I cried. When we speak on the phone, I always tell her that I love her. She is so sweet.

'I love you more,' she replies.

I couldn't love that girl any more if I had given birth to her myself. In the time that she has been around me, she has given me so much. When I die, I will leave her the beautiful Cartier ring that Ron bought for me.

I've got a home; well, it's not really a home, it's a house, a house where I store all my belongings. My sofa, my bed, all my knick-knacks, but it's not a home. The only way I can describe it is that it's like a holiday home — empty. I don't possess a saucepan or even a frying pan.

I don't need things like that. I have got a fridge but that is always empty except for two tins of Pilsner lager and they are not mine; I don't drink.

I don't go food shopping because if I buy food, more often than not I end up throwing it away. I eat take-aways, mainly.

I have got a small, white marble table. Two places are always set, but I have never eaten a meal from that table.

I turn the key in the door, and I know there is no one there waiting for me. I hate living alone.

Normality, that's what I want. A simple thing, you might say. But not for me. I really don't think I will ever achieve true contentment. But then, never say never, ever the optimist.

In the three years since Ron divorced me, life has been difficult at times. But it has also been extraordinary. Ron and I got our decree absolute in August 1994. Reading through the cold print, all I felt was an overwhelming sense of sadness. I never wanted a divorce. I felt hurt, not bitter or angry.

I just hoped that the people who had worked so hard and who had been so anxious, for their own reasons, to separate Ron and I, would now be satisfied. But what a hollow victory.

9

The Final Chapter

R on and I were divorced. Legally that is. But once a Kray always a Kray. The piece of paper said we were each our own person again, although I should have known that you're never truly free from the Krays.

Now that we were no longer man and wife, maybe the pressure would be less. Over the next few months, Ron phoned me often. He even sent me flowers. He continued asking me to visit him. My biggest regret is that I refused him — it was the only time I did. I was frightened of being sucked back into the circus and, to be honest, I'd had enough. I still loved him, but I couldn't, and wouldn't, take the crap around him.

That was in August 1994. Seven months later, in March 1995, I got a phonecall saying that Ron was seriously ill. He had been taken to Wexham Park Hospital in Slough, suffering from a heart-attack. He was 61 years old and had served 27 years of his

30-year prison sentence, most of it in Broadmoor.

When I received the phonecall, I knew that Ron must be very ill for the authorities to take him out of Broadmoor to an outside hospital.

The caller was frantic. He wanted to tell me exactly what had happened. Ron had got up in the morning, and washed and dressed as normal. The nurse unlocked his cell door. Ron asked the nurse for a light for his first cigarette of the day. Patients are not allowed matches or a lighter because of the dangerous arsonists that are housed there, which is a reasonable precaution given the circumstances. Down one side of the corridor, built into the walls, are special bricks for the nurses to strike a match against. Nurses are the only ones allowed to carry the matches — minus the box. Broadmoor rules state that the matches and the box are not to be kept together at any time in case they are stolen.

Ron took a long drag from his cigarette and stepped out of his room, he was happy enough. He started to walk along the corridor towards the day-room, even stopping to pass the time of day with another patient. Suddenly, he stumbled and fell against the wall, gasping for breath. He clutched his chest and the colour drained from his face.

Realising there was a problem, the other patient raised the alarm by shouting for help. Two nurses rushed to Ron's aid. He had stopped breathing. Anxiously, they tried to revive him. Someone shouted, 'Get a fucking ambulance.'

Inmates rushed from their cells, and the whisper went round: 'Ronnie Kray's collapsed'. The chances are that the newspapers would get hold of the story quicker than Ron would get to the hospital.

Getting an ambulance for such a high-profile prisoner is not as simple as it sounds. The authorities have to take into consideration the fact that it might be an elaborate hoax. Police and security are put on red alert. Broadmoor goes on 'lock down'. All movement inside the hospital grinds to a halt. They can't take any chances.

Back on the ward, inmates were quickly head-counted back into their cells before the ambulance was allowed to reverse up to the door. Eventually, Ron was put in the back of the ambulance. He was covered in a red blanket with an oxygen mask on his face.

Broadmoor's huge wooden gates were flung open and the ambulance swept through, sirens wailing and blue lights flashing. A helicopter hovered above the ambulance as it sped down the narrow streets. Road blocks were set up quickly and the surrounding motorways were sealed off; the security could not have been tighter even for the President of the United States. Police outriders on their motorbikes escorted the ambulance to the hospital. Inside the ambulance, paramedics were frantically working on Ron.

Doug, who was a nurse at Broadmoor, phoned me. His voice broke, and although clearly upset, he told me not to worry and not to bother going to the hospital as the security was watertight. Nobody was allowed to see Ron, not even me.

On the practical side, I knew they must have whisked Ron out of Broadmoor with no personal effects of his own. No pyjamas, no Brylcreem, no cigarettes, absolutely nothing, not even a toothbrush. As usual, all his belongings would be left behind.

When we were married, I knew the score. I would go to a shop and buy him these practical things without being asked.

Now we were no longer married, who would get him the things he needed?

These personal things were as important to Ronnie as you and I. There was no one else to get them.

I decided to go into town to buy what he needed and take them to him, not necessarily to see him, just to leave him the bits at the hospital with a note. I drove into Maidstone town centre. I nipped into Marks and Spencer's and bought him a couple of vests and a new pair of pyjamas. There was a long queue at the checkout. Anxiously, I waited to be served. It seemed like everybody wanted to pay by cheque. I was in a hurry because I wanted to get to Slough before the M25 got too busy and I still had to go home and change my clothes.

Eventually I was served, and raced home to get changed. Then it dawned on me that I had forgotten his Brylcreem. Ron was so particular he always used Brylcreem. So I stopped off at a local Spar shop to buy some. As I was walking around the shop I could hear the radio gently playing in the background. Suddenly, there was a news-flash saying, 'We interrupt this broadcast with news just in. The gangster, Ronnie Kray, is dead.'

I went numb. I did not know what to do. Ronnie. Dead? It couldn't be. They must have got it wrong. I dropped my wire shopping basket on the floor and leant against the shelves.

The lady who owned the shop approached me. She knew who I was. She had a look on her face, that look of awkwardness and pity.

'I am so sorry to hear about your sad loss ...'

I couldn't speak. I burst into tears and ran from the shop. My mind was racing. I had to get to a phone.

As I walked into my house, I could hear my phone ringing. In actual fact, it never stopped ringing. Mostly it was the Press, all wanting to know the ins and outs of Ronnie's death. Others were Ron's friends desperate for news. I just did not know what to do. So I rang Maidstone prison where Reggie is and left a message with them saying who I was and my home phone number. I wanted to speak to him. I needed to speak to him. A friend intercepted all my calls because I was too distressed even to be polite to the many callers all wanting to send their condolences.

Half-an-hour later, Reggie managed to get through to me and he was inconsolable. We were both were. Each sobbing uncontrollably, unable to speak to each other.

Through the sobs, I told Reggie that I would be going away for a couple of days. I had to. I wanted to think. I wanted to be alone. He agreed it was a good idea that I went away and didn't speak to the Press. Reggie was in prison so the Press couldn't get to him. Nobody was able to phone him either so, in a way, he was shielded from the frenzy of activity. I looked out of my window and saw the Press beginning to gather.

With the help of a friend, I gathered up a few belongings and got into my car, despite the Press, and went to Brighton for a couple of days. I walked along the sea-front on my own, desperately trying to gather my thoughts.

In a way, I blamed myself for Ron's death. If only I had been to visit him. It had been seven months since the divorce. Seven months since I had seen him. Now I would never see him again.

I think he knew that he was going to die. He had put all his affairs in order. I hadn't heard from him for two weeks, since he sent me flowers, and I had turned him down once again when he asked me to visit him. I wandered along the sea-front feeling empty. I couldn't get Ron out of my mind. If only ...

I returned home to the Press onslaught and the endless phonecalls from Ron's friends all wanting details of the funeral. When? Where? Time? Place? All questions I couldn't answer yet. I phoned Broadmoor to see if I needed to make any arrangements. They said that Reggie had it all under control.

I spoke to Ron's intensive care nurse. He was really upset that Ron had died and told me that from the day I left, he never saw Ron laugh again. He said that it seemed he had just given up on life. That really upset me.

Ron always told me how I used to make him laugh and how I was so much like his mother. I think she must have made him laugh, too. That was nice, but now I had to live with the fact that within seven months of me leaving Ron, he was dead.

And I hadn't said goodbye to him. I needed to say my final farewell. Most of all, I needed to put things straight between us.

Two days before his 'state' funeral through London's East End, I slipped quietly into the Chapel of Rest.

I was dressed in the pin-striped suit that Ron had always admired, and my eyes were shielded by Jackie O-style glasses. I took a huge wreath of white carnations and red roses with me shaped like a broken heart.

I had come to say my private goodbyes to my husband. I drove my small car through Bethnal Green.

Market traders lined the street, plying their goods as usual, their cockney accents booming over the rush-hour traffic, the banter of the EastEnders never changing. 'Git yer luvly narnas 'ere.' Life goes on.

As I approached the Chapel of Rest, I noticed a wall of photographers who had been cordoned off, opposite the entrance to the chapel. Outside stood sullen-faced security men, hands deep inside their dark overcoat pockets, all looking like the robbers' dog. I parked my car around the side of the building. Four minders were waiting for me.

Avoiding the Press cameras, they smuggled me through a side entrance and showed me into the room where Ron's body was laid out. There was a strange smell in the air, vaguely clinical, like a hospital. I will never forget that awful smell, the smell of death, it made such an impact on me. The room was cold. I shivered.

I'd never seen a dead body before and, at first, I was frightened to go up to the coffin. I took a deep breath. I pulled up a chair and sat on Ron's right side — by his good ear. He looked peaceful, but he didn't look like Ron. He had all this make-up on and he wouldn't have liked that, so I got a big bundle of tissues out of my bag and gently wiped some of it off.

Nervously, I pushed the lid of the coffin down so that I could see his hands — I always loved his hands. They were strong, masculine hands with short nails that were always scrupulously clean. Ron always said you can tell a man by his handshake. A firm handshake meant a trustworthy man.

I got out the cigarettes I'd brought with me — ten John Player Specials. Only ten because, still in my heart, I wanted him to give up smoking, knowing it was bad for him. I unwrapped the cellophane and put them in the coffin close to his right hand, within easy reach. That's what he wanted.

'Kate,' he had said, 'when I die, make sure I've got some fags with me so I can smoke them on the way to Heaven.'

I was scared to touch him at first, so I stroked his hair. They'd parted it all wrong and it wasn't Brylcreemed — Ron always liked his hair Brylcreemed. I wanted to go and get some, but I thought I had better not, so I rearranged it. I remember thinking that at least they had put his teeth in, because his face wasn't sunken. The room was filled with lovely spring flowers.

It was cool and calm and there were crucifixes on the wall, which made the memories flood back. Ron was very religious. I remember him telling me once to get him a gold cross and chain.

'And make sure you get me one with a little man on it,' he said.

He did make me laugh sometimes.

In the chapel, I didn't know what to say at first, because it was all so odd. I had lost my voice and was whispering away, so I tried to keep close to his good ear so he could hear me.

I said, 'You'd laugh if you could see all the palaver that's going on ... everyone is very upset and they are all arguing about who's going to carry your coffin.'

Once I had started talking, it became a lot easier. I sat talking to Ron for a hour. I had a lot to talk about. I told him how everyone was driving me mad. The world and his wife wanted to come to the funeral. It was pandemonium.

It was turning into a four-ringed circus. We certainly had a strong-man or two. How he would have loved all the fuss.

He often spoke of his funeral and he said he wanted to be buried the old-fashioned way, with the horses wearing plumes pulling a glass hearse. I told him I'd make sure he got what he wanted and I'd see that there was 'The Colonel' — his nickname — spelled out in chrysanthemums along the side of the hearse. He said 'smashin''.

I wanted to say my goodbyes to Ron alone. I told him I was sorry if I had done or said anything to upset him. We made our peace, and I started to cry. Ron hated women crying.

If I ever got upset on a visit, he'd get out his big white hankie and wipe my mascara all over my face so I looked like a panda. Then he would say something to try and make me laugh like, 'pack up your snivelling or I'll smack your arse!'

I like to remember him on the good visits we had — him saying 'Come on, me old Dutch, you sit by me!' And sitting outside in the summer with his shirt off, laughing.

Now he was dead, cold in his coffin. I started to cry. There was no white hankie, there was no comfort, but what happened next made me laugh.

Workmen outside of the Chapel of Rest were repairing a window. I could hear them in the background, whistling, hammering, getting on with their job. Life goes on. I was distraught. Out of the blue, one of the workmen yelled, 'Where's me fucking hammer?'

I looked at Ron and laughed. Even in death he knew the precise moment for humour. Laughter had been so important in our relationship. Against all odds, what was often called Britain's most bizarre marriage had lasted longer than five years.

So many people wanted to attend Ron's funeral that the arrangements were not going to be simple. On the day of the funeral, I was ill with the 'flu and bronchitis. My publisher's brother, David Blake, sent his stretch limo with blacked out windows and a chauffeur for my use for the day.

The question was, who was going to be my minder? Not wanting to upset anyone was hard, so I said 'Yes' to them all. There was Harry 'H' and Albert Reading in the limo. Waiting outside the church was 'Cornish' Mick and Ronnie Fields.

The arrangements were very carefully done for the funeral by a lovely lady called Flanagan, a long-term friend of the twins. Flanagan was the first Page Three girl. She is a blond bombshell even in her early 50s with a heart of gold.

On the day of Ron's funeral, it seemed that the whole of London came to a standstill. It was later described by film director Michael Winner as 'a great spectacle, equal to the Coronation or the Lord's Mayor Show.' It was heralded as the biggest funeral the country had seen since former Prime Minister Sir

Winston Churchill's in 1965, when an estimated 50,000 people turned out to pay their respects.

The service was held in St Matthew's Church, Bethnal Green, and led by Father Christopher Bedford, on Wednesday, 29 March 1995 at noon.

I arrived at the Church to be greeted by a sea of Press from all over the world. The limo pulled up in front of the gates and I stepped out to be greeted by the minders.

On the instructions of Reg, no one was allowed into the church until he had arrived because he wanted to be the first to go into the church to say his goodbyes.

When he arrived, it was complete pandemonium. He stepped from the car still handcuffed to his guards. The crowd went wild. Everyone was pushing and shoving trying to get a glimpse of him. He looked tiny compared to his guards. He tried to raise his arm to wave to the crowd, but one of the officers pulled it down. Quickly, he was whisked around to the back entrance of the church.

I looked through the glass door at the entrance of the church. I saw the saddest sight I am ever likely to see. It was Reggie Kray standing beside the coffin of his beloved twin, his head bowed, his face expressionless. He just stared at the oak coffin. He looked so alone. I wanted to break down the door and put my arms around him, just to comfort and hold him. My heart went out to him. A million thoughts must have been running through his mind. Who would he write to? Who would he argue with? Who would he love? What would he do without Ronnie? Poor Reg, I thought, how was he going to cope? He stood beside the coffin for what seemed an eternity.

Flanagan broke my thoughts as she unlocked the door. Reggie stood beside her with an outstretched hand. He shook every man's hand and kissed every lady. Reggie was very strong; he held me tight. I sobbed. He whispered in my ear. 'Now's not the time for tears — we cry later.'

He gave me his hankie and nodded his head. Just hearing his voice made me worse — he sounded just like Ron.

Flanagan showed us to our allocated seats and we all had our own service sheets with our names on them. The church was full to capacity. Flanagan had to lock the door to prevent anyone else getting in.

Needless to say, the service was very emotional but all the time I was trying to stifle my cough with lozenges and nasal sprays. A video camera panned about, zooming in for close-ups of our reactions. I found it very intrusive. Some bright spark decided it would make a good video. Even in death they wouldn't leave Ron alone. Was nothing sacred?

I tried hard not to cough and splutter but it was useless. What with me crying and coughing, all that could be heard was me barking like a seal.

My thoughts went back to when I went to pay my last respects to Ron in the Chapel of Rest. My last words to him were, 'If I was organising your funeral, I would have played the song "I Will Always Love You" by Whitney Houston.'

Nobody was in the room when I said that. Nobody except Ron, of course. He hated that sort of music. He preferred classical music, his favourite being Madam Butterfly.

The funeral service continued; it was beautiful.

Frank Sinatra sang 'My Way'. A list of names was read out of friends who were unavoidably detained, friends from Broadmoor and prisons all around the country. The hymn 'Morning Has Broken' was sung by the choir.

There was a deafening silence while a message was read out by a friend from Reggie.

'My brother Ron is now free and at peace. Ron had great humour, a vicious temper, and was kind and generous. He did it all his way but, above all, he was a man, that is how I will always remember my twin brother Ron.

'We wish for only good to come from Ron's passing away and what is about to follow is our tribute to Ron. It is a symbol of peace in that the four pall bearers will be Charlie Kray, Freddie Forman, Johnny Nash and Teddy Dennis; each one represents an area of London, North, South, East and West.'

They all encircled Ron's coffin in a minutes' silence.

Another hymn, 'Fight The Good Fight', was sung by the choir. Each of the hymns was chosen carefully and was relevant to Ron's life.

A beautiful poem was then read, one that I will always remember:

Do not stand at my grave and weep
I am not there. I do not sleep.
I am a thousand winds that blow.
I am the diamond glints on snow.
I am the sunlight on ripened grain,
I am the gentle autumn rain.
When you awaken in the morning's hush
I am the swift uplifting rush.

Of quiet birds in circled flight
I am the soft stars that shine at night.
Do not stand at my grave and cry,
I am not there; I did not die.

Up to that point, I had been trying to contain my coughing and breathing difficulties due to my bronchitis. I hadn't even looked at the service sheet. Right at the end, unbeknown to me, 'I Will Always Love You' was played and I could not contain my grief any longer. I howled, not quite believing it. Of all the songs they could have chosen, they chose that one, the one that I had told Ron about in the privacy of the Chapel of Rest.

Every gangster in the church pulled out a white handkerchief as they shed a tear. The service finished and we were ready to leave. I put my dark glasses on to hide my puffy eyes. But nothing could hide my nose; it was bigger than my hat and must have been the first bit of me to leave the church.

There were funeral cars as far as the eye could see. Ronnie's coffin was in a Victorian glass hearse drawn by six black, plumed horses. Completely taking up one side of the hearse was Reggie's floral tribute. It read: 'The other half of me'.

It was magnificent. The funeral cortège of flower-decked black limos followed directly behind the horse-drawn hearse. Reggie was in the first car. He sat in the back with two obligatory prison officers.

Thousands of people from all over the world attended. There were sightseers on rooftops, and some had shimmied up lampposts to get a better view. The streets were lined as far as the eye could see.

Reg sat in the back of the car alone, no family or friends to comfort him in his hour of need. No compassion was shown by the authorities allowing Reg to be accompanied by someone who cared.

Behind Reg's car was Charlie Kray's. Behind Charlie's was mine. On top of every car were floral tributes. Mine was a big red heart trimmed in white carnations, but I had asked the florist to tear it in half so that it resembled my broken heart. On my card I wrote, 'Tears in my eyes I can wipe away, but the pain in my heart will always stay.'

After the church service in Bethnal Green, the cortège wound its way through the East End on a two-hour journey to the cemetery in Chingford. Ron was to be buried next to his mum and dad.

There were thousands of floral tributes, including a wreath of orchids from Ronnie's friend of 30 years, *EastEnders* actress Barbara Windsor; an R-shaped wreath from singer Morrissey, who had written a song about the Krays; and a wreath from The Who's Roger Daltrey. Mourners included *EastEnders* star Patsy Palmer and Helen Keating from TV's *London's Burning*. Mourners came from every spectrum of society, from dustmen to pop singers. All had come to pay their respects to 'The Colonel'. Some had come out of curiosity.

During the journey, women were banging on the windows of the passing cortège, men were crying openly. TV crews were trying to stick their cameras in the windows of the passing limos. Some journalists were talking Chinese, some were talking with Australian accents. An entrepreneur was selling 'FREE REGGIE KRAY' T-shirts. I will never forget it.

Eventually, the cortège arrived at the graveyard.

Again, it was totally surrounded by a security cordon. Immediate family were whisked to the open grave.

Unbeknown to me, there were armed commandos positioned in the graveyard to watch my back. I heard a noise directly behind me and I turned around.

The familiar face of Bobby Wren appeared from behind a gravestone with camouflage marks on his cheeks. But this was no ordinary GI Joe, and certainly no mug. Bobby is a bit of a handful, and likes to keep a low profile. He winked at me; he meant business.

We stood around the open grave. The coffin was lowered. The vicar began to commit Ron's body to the ground.

'Earth to earth, ashes to ashes, dust to dust.'

I kissed my hand and touched the coffin as it was lowered into the ground. Little did I realise then that Ron's body was not complete — his brain had been removed ...

It was a few weeks later that I learnt from a friend the horrific truth that Home Office chiefs had secretly ordered the removal of Ron's brain. It was packed in ice and sent to a laboratory in Oxford for scientific examination.

Pathologist Dr Mufeed Ali carried out the post mortem examination and reported that Ron's brain weighed just over 2lb 8oz. At the end of his two-page report, he stated, 'Brain retained for further examination'.

I was horrified. How dare they take Ron's brain? I rang the hospital, and they tried to fob me off. Dr Ali was surprised I had found out about it. At first he said it was only a slice of his brain that been taken. But 2lb 8oz is a bloody huge slice! In the end, he had no choice but to confirm that, yes, the whole brain had been removed and sent to Oxford's special neuro-pathology unit because of Ronnie's notoriety.

He didn't see anything wrong in taking Ronnie's brain. Can you believe their nerve? How would they like it if one of their loved ones was subjected to this horrific practice without permission? I spoke to the coroner. He also said it was common practice but I have never heard anything like it before in my life. Dr Ali revealed, 'We have consultants who collect cases of interest. The results could be of vital interest to scientists who believe criminal behaviour may be brought on by chemical imbalances in our little grey cells.'

A story emerged that genius Albert Einstein's brain had been secretly pickled and studied for 40 years by a pathologist, who now keeps it in a cupboard in the hall of his Kansas home.

There was no way that a pathologist was going to keep my Ron's brain in a pickle jar in a cupboard for 40 years. Not if I had anything to do with it.

I contacted the *News of the World* who made public my findings. Their headlines on 18 February 1996 screamed THE GREAT BRAIN ROBBERY. It horrified me, but without the publicity I would have had more of a struggle on my hands to find out the exact whereabouts of the missing brain.

Thanks to the newspaper, Ron's brain was finally laid to rest with the rest of his body where it should have been in the first place.

Ron often talked about his death. He wasn't

frightened of dying, and sometimes I think he even looked forward to it. He often told me that only God could judge him. When he wrote his poems, a lot of them were about dying. These two are my favourites. The first one is called *The Troubled Mind*. I think that when Ron wrote this, he was talking about himself. It's about the hopeless souls which are trapped inside the criminally insane person's mind. I'll let you judge for yourself.

As I walk along the Broadmoor corridors
I see my fellow man, trudging the floors
Getting nowhere, like a boat with no oars.
They all have a troubled mind
Most are looking for the peace of mind
They cannot find.
Some are cruel, some are kind
God forgive them who have the troubled mind;
Only when they go to The Great Beyond,
* peace will they find.*

This second poem is called *Peace of Mind*. I asked Ron once that, if he could have one wish, what it would be. I thought his answer would be freedom, wealth, or a chance to start again to alter the outcome of his prison sentence. But no, it was none of these things.

Ron paused for a moment to think. He took a drag on his cigarette, and lent back in his chair. I looked at him. His craggy face looked tired. He sighed and said, 'If I had one wish, it would be peace of mind.'

A few days later, in the post I received this beautiful poem. I think that visit and my question prompted this poem.

> *As I ask for peace of mind*
> *And think of the sheep on the green hills*
> *And try to combat my mixed-up wills*
> *I, of God, ask for peace of mind.*
> *That, only when I take the big sleep, will I find*
> *No man knows me*
> *Only He can my mind see*
> *And with the big sleep, set me free.*

Ron was very psychic. On many of my visits to Broadmoor, he told me his innermost secrets. One was that he was convinced that every evening his mother came to him. He said he felt a presence in his cell and a comforting hand on his left shoulder. It was always the same. Ron wasn't frightened by this experience, he said he couldn't sleep until he had felt it.

It almost became an obsession with him, like the addiction of taking a sleeping pill every night. Ron was certain she had come back to watch over him as she had always done. She was especially close to Ron because he was the sickly one of the twins and nearly died from tuberculosis at an early age.

Patients who were affected by this were taken away to isolation hospitals, as it was commonly thought that fresh air, peace and quiet would help. Ron was taken to an isolation hospital in the country, but he pined for Reg and made no progress. Violet, sensing this, decided to discharge him against the doctors' better judgement.

But a mother always knows what's best for her own child. She knew in her heart that if Ronnie was back home with Reggie, it would make all the difference. She was a strong-willed woman and defied them all.

'He's coming home with me where he belongs,' she insisted. She was a 'no nonsense', East End woman. Needless to say, Ron went home.

Ron felt the presence of his mother in his cell on more than one occasion. He said that he felt his mother was reaching out from the grave to beckon him to her ... in heaven.

Ron saw nothing odd in the idea of going to Paradise. He laughed and thought of it as a 'Gangster's Paradise'.

He never showed any remorse for his crimes. He knew he did some terrible things. If you asked him whether he had viciously attacked a man with a red-hot poker, leaving his almost blind in the left eye, he would tell you the truth and freely admit it. Violet never reckoned that he was all that bad, but then mothers are like that. Ronnie said his mother once asked a prying journalist who was hoping to get an exclusive story, 'If you had to choose between your boys and the police, what choice is that; especially if that is all you've got?'

Ronnie loved his mother and felt sure he would meet her in heaven. I believe Ronnie knew, with absolute certainty, even months before he had his fatal heart-attack, that he was going to die. He put his affairs in order almost as though a doctor had told him to. He made a Will, and made sure all his financial dealings were settled, but even Ronnie's last Will and Testament was to create trouble.

On 28 September 1989, Ron had his Will drawn up. This was two months before our wedding. Just before his death in 1995, he phoned me and said that he was not going to change the contents of his Will. I never questioned him because I knew the reasons why.

When Ron had his Will drawn up, he explained to me that he was going to leave his jewellery to Reggie. Fair enough. He also explained the reasons why the remainder of his estate was to be divided between three people. Charlie Smith, who was his 'friend' in Broadmoor; Anne Glew, a close friend; and me, his wife. I was angry initially, and we had a few words. I didn't like the idea that he treated Anne Glew the same as his wife. He was adamant. After he explained his reasons I didn't argue with him. He said that the three of us, in our own way, made his life bearable. Each of us made his life complete, so when he told me after the divorce that he was not going to change his Will, I wasn't surprised.

Six months after his death, I got a phonecall from Reggie saying he was going to contest the Will. He said that I was no longer Ron's wife and I deserved nothing. I didn't argue. If that was what Reggie had decided, then so be it. It wasn't what Ron wanted. Maybe I should have told Reggie that, but then he didn't ask. I didn't want Ron's money. I didn't want his jewellery. I had what I wanted — my memories, and nobody could take them away from me, not even Reggie.

In 1997, two years after Ronnie's death, Reggie finally married his girlfriend Roberta inside Maidstone Prison. Reggie has been married before. He married a beautiful London girl called Frances Shea. Her parents did not approve of the match but, nevertheless, Reggie and Frances married on the

19 April 1965 and in Bethnal Green it was the wedding of the year. Reggie loved Frances more than life itself and when, two years later, at the tender age of 23, she committed suicide, Reggie was devastated. Much later he wrote, 'Part of me died when Frances died, and I stopped caring about things. The rest of me died when my mother passed away.'

In all honesty, I never thought Reggie would ever marry again. But after nearly 30 years in prison, maybe that was just what he needed.

Sceptics might say that the only reason he married at that late stage of his sentence was because he knew the Parole Board would look favourably on his plea for freedom if he had a wife and a stable home to go to. But knowing Reg as I do, I don't believe this for one minute.

In June 1997, Charlie Kray was jailed for twelve years for master-miding a plot to supply £39m of cocaine. It took the jury at Woolwich Crown Court 12 hours and 10 minutes of deliberation to find Charlie guilty of plotting to supply two undercover cops with five kilos of cocaine every fortnight for five years. He was also found guilty of supplying £63,000 worth of the drug.

Knowing Charlie Kray as I do, I believe a lot of what Charlie may have said to the police is utter rubbish. Although there was clearly evidence to prove Charlie's involvement in the crime, my view is that much of what Charlie said was made up in an attempt to live up to his brothers and their gangster image. Over the years, Charlie has given people what they wanted to hear from a Kray — he talked the talk and walked the walk.

I often think about my life with Ron. I might hear a song on the radio or simply be talking to a stranger in a shop when I feel his presence around me. It happens often.

But nothing prepared me for the strange dream I had in the early hours of one morning.

I woke up with a start. For a moment I had no idea where I was. I remember looking at the small alarm clock that stands on the bedside table. It was 3.35 am. I took a sip of water and lay back down. Then, suddenly, I saw my dad standing in front of me. He looked young. He was wearing his checked overcoat, the one he always wore when I was a child. I didn't understand. I was puzzled because my father had died a year before. I studied my dad's lovely face. I remember clearly asking, 'What are you doing here, Dad?'

Dad smiled. A familiar smile. One that I had missed so much.

'I wanted to see you,' he answered.

I was puzzled. 'But you are dead.'

Dad smiled and explained. He said that, yes, he was dead, but he never left me. He said that when I suddenly start thinking of him, for no reason at all, that's when he is with me. I can't usually see him but, he said, he makes himself felt inside my head.

I asked him, 'How come I can see you now?'

He answered, 'Because you are dead, too.'

At first I was shocked, then I was glad. I was with my father and I loved him.

I wanted to kiss him but I was afraid to, in case he got upset. Before his death he used to cry over the slightest little thing. But dad was happy.

' No ... no, it's all right, nobody cries here.'

So I put my arms around him and cuddled him tight. I have always maintained that is what arms are for — cuddling.

Then I saw Ron. He looked great. He was wearing a Prince of Wales checked suit. His hair was jet black. I gasped, 'Ron. You look brilliant. You look so young.'

He didn't look like the Ron I knew. He looked more like the glamorous photos I had seen of him. He laughed and explained that after death, if a spirit wants to return to their loved ones, then they usually manifest themselves in the form of when they were at their happiest. In his case, it was in the 1960s. But Ron being Ron, he wanted me to pass on a message to Reggie. I promised that I would. He said, 'Tell Reggie that I'm all right and that it is smashin' here.'

He insisted that I got the message right. As usual.

At that point, my dad told me that it was time I went back. He said that it wasn't my time yet. I didn't want to go. I wanted to stay with Ron and my dad. They said that it wasn't possible. I miss my dad so much and I know he loved me. I was his little girl and I remember that whenever I went out in the evening when I was a teenager, my dad would always leave the landing light on until I got home safely.

Dad smiled at me. He looked at peace.

'I'll leave a light on in heaven for you,' he said.

I kissed him goodbye. Then I kissed Ron.

I opened my eyes and I was back in my bed again. I sat up in bed. I wasn't frightened. I felt calm but wide awake.

This prompted me to visit Ron's grave. I hadn't been since the funeral. I drove to Chingford cemetery, taking a bunch of spring flowers with me.

I stood there at Ron's grave for five minutes, biting back the tears. I said my final goodbye, knowing he was not there.

I've never been back to Ron's grave since that April day, and I don't think I will go back again.

I know Ron is not really there. I know he is on the other side with friends who truly love him. I know, too, that he will never be forgotten. The interest in Ronnie Kray now is as great as ever, and there is one thing I know for sure — I will always be known as Kate Kray. When I'm introduced to people, it will always be: 'This is Kate. Kate Kray. Wife of ...'

*　　　　　*　　　　　*

On the 8 May 1998, Reggie completed his 30-year sentence. He applied for parole, but was refused. He is not eligible to reapply until 2001. He will be 67 years old.

Writing this book has made some kind of sense of my life. It has put it all into perspective. Ron's death was the end of an era and the close of a chapter in my life. I have now started a new chapter in a new house and am busy writing a new book about the subject I know best — Tough Guys, what else ...?

Titles Available from Blake Publishing

Lifers
by Kate Kray

Never has there been a true crime collection more chilling than this ...

Kate Kray, the beautiful wife of killer Ronnie Kray, went behind the high walls and steel bars of Britain's jails to talk with eight deadly criminals about their crimes.

Paperback £5.99

Public Enemy Number 1:
   The Life and Crimes of Kenny Noye
by Wensley Clarkson

Kenneth Noye: criminal mastermind, cop-killer and millionaire. Britain's wealthiest and deadliest villain abandoned his country estate to go on the run in 1996, after young motorist Stephen Cameron was stabbed to death on a roundabout off the M25.

Was Kenny Noye really implicated in this vicious murder? The truth is revealed by best-selling author Wensley Clarkson for the first time.

Paperback £5.99

Prices include post and packing in the UK.
Overseas and Eire, add £1.00 to the price of each book.

To order by credit card, telephone 0171 381 0666.

Alternatively, fill in the coupon below and send it,
with your cheque or postal order made payable to
Blake Publishing Limited, to:

Blake Publishing Limited
Mail Order Department
3 Bramber Court, 2 Bramber Road
London W14 9PB

Please send me a copy of each of the titles ticked below:

☐ LIFERS   £5.99

☐ PUBLIC ENEMY NUMBER 1:
    THE LIFE AND CRIMES OF KENNY NOYE
                                                        £5.99

Name...
Address...
....
....
Postcode ....

Please allow 14 days for delivery.